FINANCIAL RISK MANAGEMENT

UNIT 9

CONTINGENT RISK AND POLICY ISSUES

Financial Strategy

Prepared for the Course Team by Richard Wheatcroft
with contributions by Bernardo Bátiz-Lazo

The Open University
BUSINESS
SCHOOL

OPEN UNIVERSITY COURSE TEAM

Core Group

Professor Janette Rutterford, *Production and Presentation Course Team Co-Chair and Author*
David Barnes, *Author*
Bernardo Bátiz-Lazo, *Presentation Course Team Co-Chair and Author*
Marcus Davison, *Author*
Keith Dixon, *Author*
Graham Francis, *Author*
Carmel de Nahlik
Jan Gadella, *Author*
Margaret Greenwood
Heinz Kassier
Tony Anthoni, *Course Manager*
Clare Minchington, *Author*
Kathy Reay, *Course Team Assistant*
Pat Sucher, *Author*
Patricia Swannell, *Author*
Richard Wheatcroft, *Author*

External Assessor

Professor Paul Draper, Walter Scott and Partners Professor of Finance, University of Edinburgh

Production Team

Sylvan Bentley, *Picture Researcher*
John Bradley, *Design Group Co-ordinator*
Martin Brazier, *Graphic Designer*
Henry Dougherty, *Editor*

Jenny Edwards, *Product Quality Assistant*
Anne Faulkner, *Information Specialist*
John Garne, *Computing Consultant*
Roy Lawrance, *Graphic Artist*
David Libbert, *BBC Series Producer*
Richard Mole, *Director of Production OUBS*
Kathy Reay, *Course Team Assistant*
Linda K. Smith, *Project Controller*
Doreen Tucker, *Compositor*
Steve Wilkinson, *BBC Series Producer*

External Critical Readers

Stephen Abbott
George Buckberry
Linda Cinderey
Roland Davis
Angela Garrett
Jane Hughes
Ed Hutt
Rosemary F Johnson
Geoff Jones
Robin Joy
David Kirk
Archie McArthur
Richard Mischak
Professor Chris Napier
Eugene Power
Manvinder Singh
Tony Whitford

The Open University, Walton Hall, Milton Keynes MK7 6AA

First published 1999. Reprinted 2002

Copyright © 2000 The Open University

Edited, designed and typeset by The Open University

Printed in the United Kingdom by The Burlington Press, Foxton, Cambridge CB2 6SW

ISBN 0 7492 9788 3

Further information on Open University Business School courses may be obtained from the Course Sales Development Centre, The Open University, PO Box 222, Milton Keynes MK7 6YY (Telephone: 01908 653449)

3.4

26989B/b821b4u9i3.4

CONTENTS

1 INTRODUCTION

In this final unit of the Financial Risk Management block you will find two main themes. First, we will consider the one key aspect of risk management so far deferred: dealing with **contingent risk**. In other words, risk to which we will only become exposed if a particular event or situation happens.

We are in the realm of financial **options**, which are designed to cater for situations where the risk may crystallise or could disappear without trace. Note it is not whether the risk eventually produces a gain or a loss; it is whether the risk itself becomes an exposure for the organisation. Options are a set of financial instruments that have always been useful for managing contingent risk but which have only in recent years become amenable to analysis and accurate pricing. As with so many areas of financial engineering, the spread of dramatic amounts of powerful desktop computing has served to make practical much that was previously ignored as being of merely theoretical interest. You will not be expected to delve into the intricacies of the models produced for valuing options, but this unit is a useful opportunity for you to look inside the mysterious black boxes whose results are all too often regarded uncritically as 'holy writ'. To use a motoring analogy, you will be opening the bonnet (hood to American readers) to see that there is an engine of a certain configuration, a radiator, a starter motor and an alternator among other things. But you will not be dismantling the constituent pieces, simply investigating why they are there.

> You can consider 'contingent risk' as the label for the generalised topic and 'options' as the label for the practical implementation. In the general press you are likely to see 'options' used to mean both theory and practice.

The final theme for this block returns to the concerns of the early part of Unit 7. There we were concerned about the *policy* aspects of risk management; we discussed the concept of **risk mapping** as the analysis stage of the policy process. We can now complete the picture by looking at the rest of risk policy-setting, in essence thinking about designing a risk management *system*.

You may be relieved to note from the thickness of this unit that it is somewhat shorter than the earlier ones in this block. While this is true and intentional, so as to keep the overall time spent on Units 7 to 9 in reasonable balance with the rest of B821, this unit will not prove quite as quick to study as might be assumed from the word count. You will find some of the material quite challenging – especially some of the options work – as well as three quite 'meaty' readings and a video case study.

Aims and objectives of the unit

By the end of this unit, you should be able to:

- understand the idea of contingent risk and recognise it in management situations
- describe the main elements of a financial option contract and its uses
- describe the key factors involved in the valuation of financial options
- make use of a computer software implementation of the Merton model for valuing share options, and its equivalent model for currency options

- understand the implications of organisational strategy for risk management, and vice versa
- comprehend the workings of a risk management system and, for a reasonably straightforward situation, outline the key design elements of such a system.

2 CONTINGENT RISK

Let us begin by clarifying what we mean by 'contingent risk'. It is a risk in the usual concept used throughout Units 1 or 7, *but our exposure to contingent risk is only triggered if a particular occurrence or sequence of events transpires.* The risk exposure is contingent upon the trigger. Incidentally, the risk element itself may be 'symmetrical' or not, again using Unit 7 definitions.

This idea of 'triggering' is not as abstruse as it may at first appear. For example, let us assume a European company has submitted a tender bid for a large, overseas contract to provide a distance-learning service in Ethiopia (the bid to be in US dollars). The 'trigger' here is winning the award of the contract, which will create considerable foreign exchange risk for the organisation plus some interest risk and credit risk, the latter depending on which party is underwriting the project.

None of this risk exposure is incurred until the company is appointed as supplier. But the company was liable to *become* exposed from the moment the fixed price, non-retractable bid was submitted. The risk is *contingent* on the bidder receiving the contract, but the company must take the potential outcome into account from the moment it decides to bid. In particular, the risk needs to be taken as a factor in the pricing of the bid.

In essence the company has sold to the potential client (for no cash, if the contract is lost) an option from the date of submission until the date of acceptance or rejection. If managers decide to hedge away the risk associated with this option, the bidding company needs to buy an equivalent option itself. As you will see this may be feasible – at a price – when considering foreign exchange, interest rates, some stocks/shares, bonds and commodities. But in other situations you may simply have to acknowledge the potential outcome and accept the exposure – or be very clever.

BOX 2.1   'I NEVER BUY ANYTHING AS ESOTERIC AS OPTIONS'

It is a common misunderstanding that options are financial products only used by highly sophisticated and/or daring financial experts. In fact we all purchase and sell contingent claims as part of ordinary life and business.

If a bolt of lightning burns down your house, what do you do? If someone steals your car, what do you do? If you fall ill on an overseas trip, what do you do?

In all the above – unless you have been excessively optimistic about the slings and arrows of outrageous fortune – you get your insurance company to reimburse you for the costs you incur. And why is the company so generous? Because it is contractually bound so to do by the premium you paid before the event. For a pre-agreed amount, the insurer has committed to take over from you the risk exposure related to the relevant unhappy event, should it occur. (You did send off the premium cheque, didn't you?)

The amount you pay is related to the estimated probability of the situation transpiring, but this likelihood is usually very low for any particular individual, so the premium is (reasonably) affordable.

Insurance is, therefore, no more or less than an *out-of-the-money put option*.

Terms such as 'out-of-the-money ' and 'put option' will be defined shortly, but you can nevertheless see the point of Box 2.1: we all deal in contingent claims regularly, even if we do not call them that.

For the rest of this topic we will concentrate on financial options, but you should always bear in mind that almost all the ideas we discuss can be extrapolated to include other instruments or elements of risk.

You should also bear in mind that financial options do not exist in a vacuum. You will always find an underlying financial transaction that triggers a potential exposure to risk. Actually, this is the reason why we call options and futures **derivatives**; because to ascertain their value (or potential exposure to risk) we have to make reference to prices set up in another market. Section 3.1 will explain this idea in more detail.

3 OPTIONS

Options are financial instruments which enable contingent risk to be traded and their importance has grown explosively in the last twenty years. Before we discuss the characteristics of options in more detail, it is worth having a brief look at their history.

We will then study the language, definitions and conventions of the occasionally obscure world of options. While this will be done primarily in respect of share options, the words and meanings carry over to other forms of the instrument and to other markets where similar instruments are traded.

3.1   OPTIONS – WHERE DID THEY COME FROM?

Options trading has existed at the fringe of financial markets for a very long time, and options already had a long history when some of the pioneering academic work on the subject was developed at the end of the nineteenth century. However, the key date in their history is relatively recent: in 1973 the Chicago Board Options Exchange (CBOE) was established and became the first registered securities exchange for the trading of options.

The Chicago Board Options Exchange

It is no coincidence that this was done in Chicago, where futures trading had already been undertaken for many years, since essentially the same systems and practices as for futures were used. In particular, a clearing house was set up for options contracts, so that options could be freely traded without concern about the ability or willingness of the other party to each transaction to pay up; this is almost identical to the method used for futures, which you read about in Unit 7.

The CBOE started modestly, only trading call options on sixteen shares in major companies quoted on the New York Stock Exchange (the terminology is explained more fully in Section 3.2). The volume and range of its option products expanded rapidly. A number of other US exchanges began trading in options and, in 1977, put options were introduced on all of them. The volume of trading grew to such an extent within the ten years from 1973, the amount of trading in options on shares often exceeded that of the underlying shares on the New York Stock Exchange.

The formal definitions of put and call options are given at the beginning of the next sub-section. For this introduction you need only realise that they are products for managing contingent risk, in a similar manner to how, in Unit 7, we used interest futures to help manage interest risk.

As a result of this success, the range of securities on which options were traded was gradually extended to options on stock indices, foreign currencies, government fixed-interest securities – even options based on the right to buy (or sell, if a put) a futures contract, for example stock index futures and commodity futures. Also, following the US pattern, options exchanges were opened in other major financial centres, for example, London, Tokyo, Singapore, Amsterdam, Paris, Frankfurt.

Another parallel development has been the growth of the 'over-the-counter' market, mainly through banks offering corporate customers options specially tailored to their needs. This market is very much assisted by the fact that both banks and their customers can check prices against securities which are openly traded. This is directly analogous to the exchange-traded interest futures and 'OTC' FRAs we discussed in Unit 7.

The four main kinds of financial options are:

- options on shares
- options on interest rates
- options on currencies
- options on commodities (e.g. metals or agricultural crops).

Our approach here will be to describe in some detail the first type of option, options on a listed share, and then extrapolate the principles derived to other types of option.

3.2   OPTIONS ON SHARES

Option dealing has its own special language, and you need to become familiar with a few terms to be able to use options. Starting with a definition for call and put options on shares, we have:

> A **call option** is a **contract** giving its owner the right (but not the obligation) to *buy* a given number of shares at a *fixed price* at any time on or before a *given date*.

> A **put option** is a contract giving its owner the right (but not the obligation) to *sell* a given number of shares at a *fixed price* at any time on or before a *given date*.

In the definition note the term '... at any time *on or before* a given date'. Strictly speaking, there are two types of option: an **American option** can be exercised 'on or before' the expiry date; a **European option** can only be exercised 'on' the expiry date. This is seldom a practical concern since, as we will see later, it is very unlikely that it is better to exercise an option early rather than keep it to expiry, or to sell it on as an unexercised option. Thus we can usually just talk about 'an option' rather than always having to add the American/European descriptor – but you ought to remember the difference so that the terminology is not confusing when encountered. Incidentally, the words came into use simply because, as you may have guessed, the common practice for option contracts differed on the two sides of the Atlantic.

We will concentrate for the moment on *call* options because many of the principles are similar for both calls and puts, but it keeps the argument clearer to look at just one version. 'Puts' will be discussed more completely in Section 4, but it was felt important to give you here the definition of a put option.

To make the discussion rather more specific, it is useful to look at the options report (for LIFFE equity options) given daily by the *Financial Times*. For 11 November 1997, it gave the following information in the overall table of option values, as shown in Table 3.1.

Table 3.1   Cable & Wireless call option prices

		Pence per share		
		Jan	Apr	Jul
C&W	460	40.5	64	73
(*479.5)	500	24.5	45	54

* Current share price

The conventions of the market are that all the quoted figures are in pence, so the table is interpreted as follows. The share is Cable & Wireless, then standing at 479.5p a share; the first column indicates the fixed price for the share for the particular option (or **exercise price** (EP)); the top row gives the *expiry date* in a short form since the July expiry date, for example, is a specified day – the third Wednesday of the month; and the body of the table gives the premium to be paid for that particular call option.

To take a particular example, if Frances Spencer decides to buy a contract (the unit of dealing, which is 1,000 shares in Cable & Wireless) of July 460 calls, she pays 73p a share, or £730 (1,000 × 73p). For this she purchases the right (but not the obligation) to buy 1,000 shares in Cable & Wireless at any time up to the expiry date in July at a fixed price of 460p a share: if she does so she is said to *exercise* the option. Alternatively, she can sell her option in the market at prevailing prices at any time up to the expiry date. If she neither sells nor exercises (as, for instance, could happen if the share abruptly fell to less than 460p and stayed there), then she would let the option *lapse* at the expiry date; that is, give it up as worthless.

There are two parties to every option, a buyer and a seller (the latter known as the **writer**). The buyer pays the premium which the writer receives, and for this the writer does have an obligation: to provide the shares at the exercise price if the buyer chooses to exercise.

Frances' profit or loss position on the expiry date, if she still holds the contract, can be set out as in Table 3.2.

Table 3.2   Profit on expiry of call option

Share price at expiry date (p)	Gross profit per share (p)	Net profit per share (p)
400	0	−73
450	0	−73
500	40	−33
550	90	17
600	140	67
700	240	167

Remember, Frances paid 73p a share per stock option.

The position at the expiry date clearly depends on what the share price is at that time. Frances has the right to buy shares at 460p and will only do so if the share price is above the exercise price of 460p; so, if the share price on expiry is less than or equal to 460p, as in the first two rows of Table 3.2, she will let the option lapse. If the share price is above her exercise price, she will buy the shares at 460p and sell them at the market price, the difference being her gross realised profit. The net profit is thus the gross profit *minus* the premium she initially paid for the option.

Of course, Frances may choose to hold on to the shares, in which case the figures are the same but the profit would not be realised.

Exercise 3.1

What would the net profit or loss position on expiry be for an investor who bought a call option on 1,000 shares with a premium of 35p and an exercise price of 600p, if the share price at expiry was:

(i)   550?

(ii) 600?

(iii) 650?

Note that the choice of exercise price does not really depend on the current share price; one can have options where the EP is below, equal to or above the current market price and the premium varies accordingly. If the EP of a call option is lower than the current share price the option is said to have **intrinsic value** – i.e. it would already make a gross profit if exercised immediately. Such a contract would be referred to as **in the money**, and call option contracts with EP equal to or above the current price are **at the money** or **out of the money**, respectively. Figure 3.1 shows the typical shape of the value of a call option before expiry, and illustrates the meaning of the terms intrinsic value and out/at/in the money.

The terms value, price, premium and cost are used interchangeably when considering options.

The dotted line shows potential profits while the solid line the net value of the option. The net value is concave because of a funny effect introduced by time to expiry. But you need not worry about that effect.

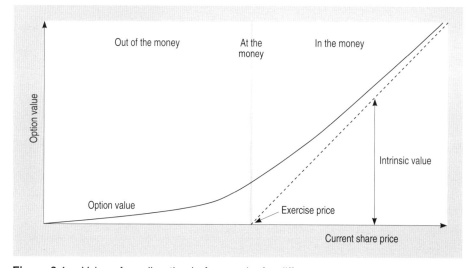

Figure 3.1   Value of a call option before expiry for different current share prices

Returning to the Cable & Wireless example, why should Frances wish to spend £730 to buy this contract? One reason could be caution: although she could lose money on her investment, the worst that could happen is that she lost the whole of the £730, but since £730 is the maximum possible loss she has limited risk. This maximum possible loss is because buying a call option gives the *right* (to exercise or sell) but *no obligation* and is the main difference between the buying of options and the buying of forwards or futures, where the only way to limit losses is to get out of the contract. This feature of call options is important in **portfolio insurance** and **guaranteed funds**, which use options to guarantee a minimum value or return on a portfolio and hence offer limited downside risk for investors.

Another reason for buying a call option on Cable & Wireless is that, if the share price goes up, the *percentage* return is much greater on the option than on an investment in the underlying shares. Suppose, for instance, that Cable & Wireless shares are at 700p on the expiry date in July. At that time Frances would exercise her option at 460p a share, giving a gross profit of 240p per share, equivalent to a pre-tax return of (240–73)/73 or 129% on her initial investment. If, on the other hand, she had invested directly in the shares at the price of 479.5p and then sold them at 700p, her gross return would be (700–479.5)/479.5 or 46% on the initial investment. Thus, options give a much higher *percentage* return than buying the shares directly if the share price goes above a certain level. Conversely, of course, percentage losses are higher with options than with shares, but with the safeguard that no more than the original option investment in value terms can be lost.

Where does this gearing effect come from? If we consider in-the-money calls, we can see from Figure 3.1 that the graph of the option value is getting closer and closer to a 45° line. This means that the value of the call begins to rise or fall at only a little bit less than the '1-for-1' rate (i.e. 1p profit/loss per 1p rise/fall in share price) we would be exposed to if we had bought the share itself. But we have only paid out the cost of the premium, a much smaller amount than would have been required to purchase the share itself. Thus the rate of change in profit or loss is geared up. For out-of-the money options the value graph rises or falls more slowly (the curve is much flatter), but the investment required to buy the option is also small, so the rate of change in investment is also relatively rapid. Indeed, in terms of 'percentage of investment' out of the money options can prove to be even more highly geared, because the premium paid is so small (compared to that for an at- or in-the-money option).

Thus, buying a call option gives a much higher percentage profit (or loss) than investing directly in the shares, and in that respect is similar to buying shares partly with borrowed money, which would also 'gear up' one's returns. However, the maximum amount of loss that can occur is limited to the initial premium.

SUMMARY

This section began with a brief look at the history of financial options; you will recall that you first met the idea of contingent claim in Unit 1. Following the discussion about futures in Unit 7, you read about how exchange-traded options operate within the system of standardised contracts, clearing houses and margins.

We then defined more exactly what is meant by call and put options, together with a number of crucial terms associated with these instruments. Please ensure that you are comfortable with the meaning of terms such as 'out of the money' and 'intrinsic value'. It would also be a good idea to remember the basic shape of the curve shown in Figure 3.1, i.e. a smooth curve that tends towards the horizontal on the left and a 45° line on the right.

Unusually, let us end this summary with an exercise, which should confirm to you that you have grasped the meaning of the option value graph.

Exercise 3.2 _____

The curve shown in Figure 3.1 is the generic shape for a call option. What would the equivalent curve look like for a put option?

Strictly speaking, the 'loss' here is only the loss due to adverse market movement; transaction costs (i.e. broker's commission and/or a 'bid–ask' spread) would also be incurred, but the premium is usually a much bigger component of total cost.

4 ANALYSING OPTIONS

The next two sections will be the most technical of this unit, dealing as they do with practical and theoretical aspects of the analysis and valuation of options. You will not be asked to go into the mathematical details of option theory – it gets quite abstruse and involved – but you will be expected to understand how to make *use* of the models.

We build up to this in three stages. To begin with, we investigate a very useful graphical technique called pay-off diagrams; this looks at the value of an option on the expiry date, and is of great practical use for anyone using options, particularly for hedging purposes. The intention is that you start to get a 'feel' for what an option is worth at the end of its life, i.e. when it becomes certain whether or not you should exercise your rights.

We then discuss how to put maximum and minimum boundaries around such values. This is essentially a qualitative analysis, but it will help the following discussion about the variables involved, and why it is they (and not others) which are included.

You have an option valuation software on your B821 disk. You also have the EQOP spreadsheet to value equity options and CURROP to value currency options.

Finally, we look at and make use of the most important option valuation model currently used: the Black–Scholes equation for valuing share options. We will discuss this model and use it directly to estimate the value of share options. We will also use the Black–Scholes model indirectly through two offsprings. First, the Merton equation to value equity options and currencies. Second, value currency options through the Garman-Kohlhagen equation.

In practice, if you ever need to calculate the value of an option, you will most likely simply plug in the variable numbers to a special calculator or spreadsheet, and read off the answer. But understanding *why* you input those particular variables will give you a good chance of spotting whether or not the answer is realistic or completely ridiculous. In the latter case, rechecking the input and output would be a good idea!

4.1 PAY-OFF DIAGRAMS

We will now look at a technique for analysing the range of profit or loss associated with an investment or hedge package, namely that of **pay-off diagrams**. These do not do anything that cannot be done in other ways, but they are designed to make assimilation of the information dramatically easier than staring at a table of numbers.

Pay-off diagrams give in graphical form the results of a transaction at the expiry date, and are an extremely useful tool of analysis. Figure 4.1 shows, in the left-hand diagram, the net pay-offs for the buyer of a call against the share price at expiry – this is the graphical form of Table 3.2. In the right-hand diagram it gives the net pay-offs for the seller or writer of the call, which is the same graph with the signs reversed. This means that if the net pay-off for the buyer is positive at a certain share price, it is exactly the same amount but negative for the writer, and if it is negative for the buyer it is the same amount but positive for the writer. In other words, the buyer's profit is the writer's loss, and vice versa.

Looking at Figure 4.1, it is clear that writing call options is extremely risky, since the potential for losses is unlimited: the more the share price rises, the bigger the writer's loss. On the other hand, this is no riskier than having sold **short** the share; in such a case you would also lose significantly if the share rose in value.

It makes a difference, however, as we shall shortly show, whether the writer also possesses the shares on which the call is written (it is then known as a **covered call**) or if he or she does not, as in the pay-off diagram, when it is known as a **naked** call.

Short selling is the practice of selling something that one does not own, hoping to buy it back more cheaply later when (and if!) the price has fallen. Some markets allow short selling, others do not.

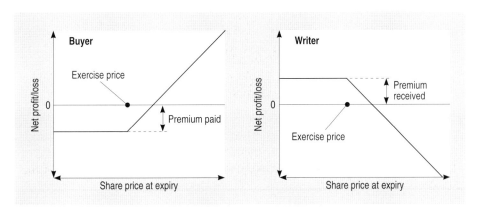

Figure 4.1   Call option: net pay-off at expiry (net of initial premium)

Activity 4.1 _____

These pay-off diagrams are all made up of straight lines, so where has the option-value curve of Figure 3.1 gone?

Pay-off diagrams show the net profit or loss from an option at the date of expiry. The curve in Figure 3.1 shows the value of an option at some time before expiry. Thus Figure 3.1 will look more and more like the left-hand diagram on Figure 4.1 as the time to expiry gets shorter.

One of the great strengths of pay-off diagrams is that they can set out the position for a complex investment by adding the diagrams of the components. Thus, Figure 4.2 (overleaf) shows, for a covered call, the diagrams for owning the share and for selling a call, and the resulting combined position. The combined position is arrived at by the following procedure: for a fixed set of share prices on expiry, the corresponding net profits for (i) the written call and (ii) the net profit on buying the shares are calculated and then the two figures are added together to give the combined net profit.

Remember, *writing* a call is the same as *selling* a call.

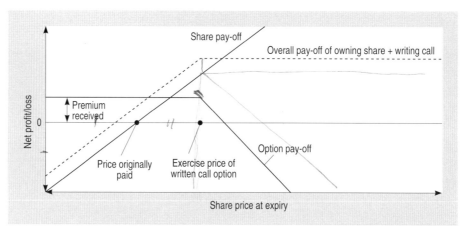

Figure 4.2 Writing a 'covered call'

On looking at Figure 4.2, which shows the net pay-offs for writing a covered call, it is easy to see why many fund managers are tempted to use this strategy: the claim is that if the share price stays below the exercise price, the fund manager retains the shares, collects the dividends, and also receives the call premium; if the share goes above the exercise price, the fund manager collects the exercise price and the premium and may or may not get the dividends (depending on when the call is exercised). In short, it is claimed to be a prudent policy if the fund manager feels that the share price is likely to fall or stay flat. Mind you, if they are proved wrong and the price rises, then the portfolio loses the gains it could have expected from continuing to hold the share without writing the option. As we will see shortly, a 'covered call' is nothing more than a put. Whether or not it is appropriate for the fund to write puts, the pretence that a covered call is somehow safe is a dangerous fiction.

We now turn our attention to the other kind of option just mentioned: the put option. Remember that the definition of a put is:

> A contract giving its owner the right (but not the obligation) to *sell* a given number of shares at a *fixed price* at any time on or before a *given date*.

The put option, by fixing the selling price, is an important tool for hedging against a fall in the market. While both buying a share and buying a call option enable investors to profit from a *rise* in the price, it is only the put option that enables them to profit from a *fall*, unless they are lucky enough to be dealing in a market and instrument that allows for short selling. For example, Eurobonds do permit 'shorting' but most stock markets do not (legitimately, anyway). In any event, even in those markets which can arrange for short sales, it is usually a relatively expensive thing to do in terms of transaction costs.

The position at the expiry date can be charted for the put in a similar way to that which we produced for the call. Suppose that, on 11 November 1997 (taken from the same *Financial Times* issue that was used for the call options), the price of a July 460 put on a Cable & Wireless share was 41.5p, then the profit/loss table is as shown in Table 4.1.

From the table we can see that above the exercise price the end-value is given by a horizontal line at −41.5, and that below the exercise price the value of the option *rises* 50p for every 50p *fall* in the share price. We can generalise this to draw the typical net pay-off diagrams for buying or writing a put, as illustrated in Figure 4.3.

Major stock markets (such as those in New York, London or Frankfurt) allow short selling of share stocks, because the profit potential of volume transactions compensates the costs of setting up the trade.

Table 4.1 Profit per share on expiry of put option

Share price at expiry date (p)	Gross profit (p)	Net profit (p)
300	160	118.5
350	110	68.5
400	60	18.5
450	10	−31.5
500	0	−41.5
550	0	−41.5

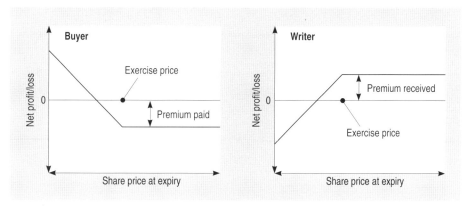

Figure 4.3 Puts: net pay-off at expiry (net of initial premium)

Buying (or selling) an appropriate number of shares, and calls and puts (with possibly different exercise prices), can be designed to give a particular combination which professional investors may use to back their views about where the share is going. To each combination there is a net pay-off diagram which can be derived – spreadsheet packages can quickly display these graphs. Many of the combinations which are widely used have commonly accepted names, and we illustrate just two of these to give an idea of the possible range.

Figure 4.4 illustrates a 'straddle', where a call and a put of the same exercise price and same expiry date are bought for one share. An investor who buys a straddle expects the share price to move substantially before expiry, either up or down. Note that he is not guessing in which direction the share price will move, simply that it will end up substantially different from the present figure – a bet on volatility.

Go to the option valuation software on your B821 disk. In the menu select *Demo* and see the effect on the straddle graph of changing the suggested parameters.

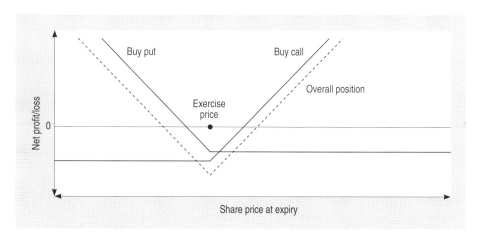

Figure 4.4 A straddle

Figure 4.5 illustrates a 'butterfly spread' where two calls are written on the same share and for the same expiry date at an exercise price as near as possible to the current share price, and a call option equally spaced on each side of this exercise price is bought. In other words, one writes two calls at an exercise price (A + B)/2 and buys one call with exercise price (B) and one call with exercise price (A).

Remember, the straddle demo in the option valuation software was designed to illustrate only buying calls and/or buying puts.

In the Cable & Wireless example above, this spread could be obtained, for instance, by writing two July 500 calls (at 54p each, thus receiving 108p) and buying the July 460 (at 73p) and the July 540 (at 43p). Notionally, the cost of the combination would thus be: 73 + 43 − 108 = 8p or £80 for the four contracts. This is notional because the table gives buying prices, and selling prices are lower, so that you would not be able to write at 54p, giving a slightly higher overall cost. This butterfly spread pays off if, as appears from the figure, the price of the shares moves only within a narrow range until the expiry date.

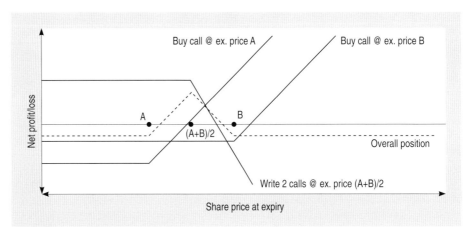

Figure 4.5 A butterfly spread

Here the view of the investor must be the opposite of that taken for the straddle. In that situation profit was made if the share price moved a lot; for the butterfly spread money is earned if the share stays close to the current price, i.e. exhibits very low volatility.

Exercise 4.1

Using the information provided for Cable & Wireless in Figure 4.5, construct a table showing the net profit per share on expiry of the options if the share price at expiry is 440p, 460p, 480p, 500p, 520p, 540p and 560p.

BOX 4.1 VOLATILE OR NOT VOLATILE, THAT IS THE QUESTION...

As we will see shortly, the value of an option depends crucially on the expected price volatility of the underlying share (or forex rate or interest rate or other rate). For both butterflies and straddles the volatility play is based on comparing the investor's – more realistically, the speculator's – view of *future* volatility with the market's opinion.

If the market's quotes of option premiums are 'fair' – and the working of supply and demand would lead us to expect that they would be – then built into each price is the market participants' average expectation of future volatility. If the investor is of the opinion that volatility will actually prove to be *higher* than this implied volatility, then it is sensible for him to buy a straddle; if he believes that future movements will be smaller than the market's expectation, he should buy a butterfly.

As always, the speculator is betting his prediction against the average expectation of the other market players.

Activity 4.2

Box 4.1 points out that straddles and butterflies are ways of exploiting a difference between the view of volatility taken by the market and by the investor/speculator. But, more fundamentally, what is the attitude of option users towards volatility – which we have come to equate with risk?

Consider two shares, Lo and Hi. Lo is a very safe share with low volatility of its share price; Hi, on the other hand, suffers a very volatile share price because it is a hi-tech business with very little current revenue but very exciting prospects (according to the management, at least!). Coincidentally, Hi and Lo happen today to have an identical share price of 500p.

You look at the premium cost of buying a three-month call option for either Hi or Lo, both with an exercise price of 500p. Which option do you think would cost you more?

It may seem peculiar, but the option for Hi will be worth more than that for Lo, even though – no, precisely because – it is more risky. In the world of options, volatility is good. Why? Because the fact that one has the downside protection of choosing not to exercise the option reduces the bad side of volatility. The upside potential remains, however, and the more volatile – the riskier – the share price, the greater the possible rise in share price.

Try following this example using the straddle example in the option valuation software. Set the strike price and current price to 500.

If you were able to answer Activity 4.2 correctly you are beginning to acquire a good 'feel' for the concept of options; if, on the other hand, you used the more normal idea that risk (i.e. volatility) is bad, just remember that the shape of an option's pay-off diagram is fundamentally different from that for buying or selling the underlying share, and the difference is profound. Section 4.2 should help everyone to come to terms with this difference between options and 'ordinary' risk management products.

Exercise 4.2

Draw the net pay-off diagram for a position which involves buying a Jul 460 call option at 73p and writing a Jul 500 call option at 54p.

Combinations of options, such as straddles and butterfly spreads, are usually only of interest to institutional investors or traders, but, in an active market, such trades benefit everybody, since, if the price of an option relative to other options or to the underlying security goes out of line (being either too dear or too cheap), then traders would see the opportunity to benefit from the mis-pricing and eventually, by doing combination trades, cause the price to move to its proper level.

There are an infinite number of option combinations which can be created. For example, straddles and butterfly spreads can be bought *or* sold, depending on the investor's view of likely price movements. Using puts and calls, bought or written, various exercise prices, plus **long** or short holdings of the shares, it is surprising how varied can be the final pay-off positions. With ingenuity it is usually possible – at a price – to 'engineer' a pay-off to suit almost any hedge or investment profile.

Of course, there is the proviso that you never find the 'golden pay-off' strategy, with a profit whatever the final share price. Strictly speaking, we should add 'for any significant period of time' to the preceding sentence – because an arbitrage situation *can* appear for a short time but does not last long enough for anyone but full-time 'market-watchers' to exploit.

Having just warned you of the crucial difference between options and, say, futures or forwards, this is an example of a similarity between the product types. The concept of an arbitrage situation – creating a risk-free profit but then it disappearing rapidly as the first people to notice exploit the opportunity – applies to all financial markets, 'normal' or derivatives. This idea of arbitrages will help us to investigate the factors influencing option values in the next sub-section.

This is the last time we will imply that derivatives are not 'normal' financial instruments. They are *different* but just as normal – or just as odd – as the other instruments we have been investigating in B821. They are, perhaps, as yet a little less common.

4.2   ARBITRAGE AND FREE LUNCHES

Table 4.2 shows the prices or premiums of twelve call and put options for Cable & Wireless. Since all these options are just different ways of taking a view on a single share price, it is only reasonable to think that there must be some relationships between the option prices. Looking more closely at the table we can see, for example, that call option prices decrease as the exercise price increases and that call option prices increase as the time to expiry increases. We now show that these two characteristics of option prices are not peculiar to Cable & Wireless but hold for all call options. We also give some other properties of call option prices, and then investigate the connection between put and call options.

Table 4.2 LIFFE option premiums, C&W, for 11 November 1997			
Current share price: 479.5p			
	Exercise price	**460p**	**500p**
Calls:	Jan '98	40.5	24.5
	Apr '98	64.0	45.0
	Jul '98	73.0	54.0
Puts:	Jan '98	21.5	42.5
	Apr '98	30.5	50.5
	Jul '98	41.5	62.0

The technique we use is to explore arbitrage possibilities inherent in combinations of options which traders could use to make risk-free profits. In practice, as mentioned in the 'golden pay-off' comment above, any mis-pricings of options which allowed such arbitrages could not last long in a liquid market – they would very soon be traded away.

An arbitrage opportunity, as you will recall from Unit 7, Section 6.2, is defined as a situation where a riskless profit can be made by exploiting different prices for the same product. An arbitrage yields a positive amount immediately and also yields non-negative amounts in the future under all possible circumstances.

In this definition 'non-negative' is a shorthand expression for either positive or zero, i.e. the investor will not have to pay any more. If arbitrage opportunities persisted, something could in effect be acquired for nothing and, in real life, there are seldom 'free lunches' on offer long enough for the average person to eat his fill.

The following propositions are examples of what can be proved if we assume there can be no free lunches; this is not in contradiction of earlier comments about arbitrages, rather it simply acknowledges that any arbitrage opportunity will usually have been eroded to nothing by exploitation long before the 'normal' investor has a chance to benefit.

So as not to disturb the flow of the discussion, the proofs for all the propositions are gathered together in the Appendix to this unit. You may well feel that the validity of some of the propositions is straightforward or intuitive, others you may feel less confident about accepting on trust. In the latter cases, do please look at the relevant part of the Appendix.

Proposition 1

The price of a call option is:

(i)   less than or equal to the current price of the underlying security;

(ii) greater than or equal to the difference between the price of the underlying security and the exercise price;

(iii) non-negative.

Or in mathematical terms:

$$S \geqslant C \geqslant \max(0, S - K)$$

where $\max(0, S - K)$ denotes the maximum of 0 and $(S - K)$; S = current share price; C = call price; K = exercise price.

Activity 4.3

Parts (i) and (ii) of this proposition are proved in the Appendix, but please prove the third part of the proposition yourself, that the call option price is always non-negative. As a hint, think about what would happen if the value *were* negative, i.e. someone had to pay you to accept a call option.

If C is negative you can earn a risk-free profit by buying the call and holding it to expiry. This gives a positive amount now and a non-negative amount later, because you can just let the option expire if it is not in profit at expiry. Thus one has a 'free lunch', which is not allowed. So the initial premise that C can be negative must be wrong; so C must be non-negative.

Activity 4.4

From Table 4.2 for Cable & Wireless call options, check that the relations in Proposition 1 hold for the Jul 460 and Jul 500 call prices.

For the Jul 460 call, the above proposition states:

479.5 ⩾ 73 ⩾ (479.5 − 460 = 19.5). These are all true.

For the Jul 500 call, the relations are:

479.5 ⩾ 54 ⩾ 0. These are all true.

Note here that when the exercise price is greater than the share price, then the difference is negative, and the lower bound on the call option value just says that the call price is non-negative.

Proposition 2

The price of a call option increases as the time to expiry increases, for the same exercise price.

Proposition 3

For the same expiry date, the prices of call options decrease as their exercise prices increase.

Exercise 4.3

Imagine it is 21 August 1999 and Aardvark International shares are trading at 238p. The following table gives the prices for call options on Aardvark. Can you spot a number of contradictions of the arbitrage conditions and devise trades that would ensure a risk-free profit?

Exercise price (p)		Call premium (p)	
	Nov	Feb	May
240	250	21	35
260	8	25	27
280	−3	17	12

American and European options

Before we give our next results for arbitrage and before we turn our attention to valuation models for options, some further option definitions are needed. Virtually all traded options are American, which, as you will recall, means they can be exercised at any time up to the expiry date, so that the buyer of the option can obtain the share (for a call) or sell it (for a put) at any point of time in this range; further, the majority of shares on which options are traded have one or more dates where they go ex-dividend up to the expiry date. This can affect the exercise decision since option holders *do not* receive dividends. So, American options are complex because the decision whether to exercise or not has to be borne in mind at every instant between purchase and expiry.

Let us illustrate this through an example: think that in May you purchase two European call options on shares of Tony's Bank plc. One expires in June and the other in September. The options are otherwise identical.

At the end of July comes the announcement that Leo Anthoni, Tony's Bank general manager, is responsible for a substantial improvement in August's annual dividend pay out. Had you exercised in June and kept the shares, then you receive the dividend windfall. But your September option will miss the dividend: because it is European, this option can't be exercised before maturity.

When purchasing your options in May, the market knows that, regardless of the dividend's actual value, the holder of September options will miss receiving the dividend. Therefore, the value of the September European option will be less than the value of the June European option. Whereas the September American option will be worth more than the June American option (i.e. proposition 2 will strictly hold for American options), as it can be exercised in June/July and receive the dividend or be kept until maturity. As a result, the need to bear in mind the possibility of early exercise makes the pricing of American options more intricate than pricing European options.

It should now be clear to you the reason why studies usually deal with European options, which can only be exercised at the expiry date, and assume that European options are on shares which pay no dividends, avoiding the problem of early exercise completely.

Incidentally the names American and European options, although traditional, are these days quite misleading: virtually all options on both American and European exchanges are in fact American.

An important result relating the values of American options to the values of the simpler European options is now given.

Proposition 4

If there is no ex-dividend date until after the time to expiry, American call options should not be exercised until expiry, and the value of an American call option is the same as that of an equivalent European call option.

This proposition is very important because it shows that valuing, in certain circumstances, the much simpler European call option (as is done, for instance in the most widely used Black–Scholes model) leads to the valuation of the equivalent American call option.

Finally, one of the most famous relations in option theory is given, the so-called **put–call parity relationship**. This proposition establishes that, if call options can be valued, the value of the equivalent put option can be found by using a simple relationship.

Proposition 5 (put–call parity)

For European options without dividends, the value of a put option is equal to the value of an otherwise identical call option minus the current share price plus the present value of the exercise price (PV(K)) for the put (or the call), i.e.

$$P = C - S + PV(K)$$

A further exploration of put–call parity is contained in *Vital Statistics*, Section 5.7.3.

So, once the value of a call option or a put option is known, the value of the other (provided it has the same exercise price and time to expiry) can be found from Proposition 5.

A proof of this relationship is given in the Appendix, but its validity can be seen almost immediately by looking at pay-off diagrams, as in Section 4.1.

Exercise 4.4

Draw the resulting pay-off diagram for owning a call and writing a put, both with the same expiry and exercise price. What does the net position resemble?

Activity 4.5

A so-called 'money-back' fund may have the following rules: investment is for a year, and the investor is guaranteed to get her money back at the end of that time. Thus, she runs no risk on her principal, and if the stock index rises she will also get some gain. How would you design such a fund? Assume that current interest rates are 10%.

If the interest rate is 10%, then £90.91 invested now becomes £100 at the end of the year. So invest £90.91 in one-year low-risk interest instruments (e.g. short-dated bonds or bank deposits) and the remaining £9.09 in a stock index option with expiry at the end of the year and exercise price at the current level of the index: this gives the fund a guaranteed £100 at year-end, plus the chance of a gain if the index rises.

"Do you ever try to explain to your kid that you spend all day buying and selling things that you don't have?"

Notice that we have concentrated on looking at call options rather than put options. This is because Proposition 5, the put–call parity relationship, enables us easily to value a put option once we have valued the equivalent call option. For example, it can also be shown that the value of a put option must be positive and that it increases with both time to expiry and with exercise price. Unfortunately, Proposition 4 does not hold for put options so that the value of an American put option may be greater than that of a European one even ignoring the additional complexity of dividends, requiring a more complex method of valuation for American put options than for American call options. In the next section, we turn to using arbitrage arguments to value European calls with no dividends more accurately.

Let us conclude this sub-section with a consolidated list of the propositions; this will prove useful for reference when we look at the variables involved in option valuation. Note that these summary versions are shortened, and for the full text you should still refer to the original entries.

Proposition 1

$$S \geqslant C \geqslant \max (0, S - K)$$

Proposition 2

The price of a call option increases as the time to expiry increases.

Proposition 3

The prices of call options decrease as their exercise prices increase.

Proposition 4

Value of American call option = value of European call option.

Proposition 5

$$P = C - S + PV(K)$$

SUMMARY

This section is the first of two containing the core material in the block concerning the practical aspects of managing contingent risk. We began with the seemingly simplistic but very powerful technique of pay-off diagrams. Since there are essentially only six shapes (i.e. buy or sell a put or call, plus buy or sell the underlying instrument), the method is indeed *simple* but it is not actually simplistic. Crucially, using the concept one can easily work out the potential outcome for *any* portfolio of options and underlying instruments. Being able to use pay-off diagrams is a skill that one may only use from time to time, but when it is needed it repays abundantly the time spent understanding the technique.

We then moved on to discussing some of the key attributes of options and their values; in particular, always remember the idea of put–call parity: it makes some seemingly silly behaviour rational. For example, if the customer and the trader both believe a share is going to rise, why would the latter be happy to buy a *put* option from the former? Because she can convert the put into a call by put–call parity.

The next section will build on the work of this one to investigate the key practical consideration one needs if one is to make good use of options: namely, how to value them. Pay-off diagrams are extremely useful in helping a manager to decide what combination of products to use to meet the objective, but then one needs a robust way of estimating a fair price for the options identified. Within known limitations, we now have such a method of valuation – the Black–Scholes model.

5 OPTION VALUATION

The course website has a link to the transcript of a TV programme on the importance of the Black–Scholes formula.

In this section, we reach the culmination of our investigation of options: valuing them. The main valuation model we will look at is called **Black–Scholes** but we will also investigate briefly another approach: the **binomial model**.

Both of these are designed primarily with share option valuation in mind, but the principles involved are much more general. We will show this when looking at the **Merton** model or the principal variation of the Black–Scholes equations to value share options. We will then move on to value currency options. We will discuss how to apply the Merton model to value currency options as well as another variant of Black–Scholes designed to value currency options. This is known as the **Garman–Kohlhagen** model after the researchers who made the adaptation from shares to currencies.

The section concludes with a number of examples, some worked out here in the text and others contained in two articles containing mini-case studies which you will find in the Course Reader.

5.1 VALUING OPTIONS ON SHARES

Myron Scholes receiving his Nobel Prize in 1997

A considerable number of attempts have been made to produce a formula which could value call or put options on shares. A radically new approach was adopted by Fischer Black and Myron Scholes in their seminal paper of 1973: their valuation model only required observable quantities to be measured to give the call or put value – in particular it needed no information on the investor's view of the likely return on the stock or on his attitude towards risk. The Black–Scholes model quickly became a success both among professional investors and the academic community, and has retained its place ever since as the most popular tool for valuing options.

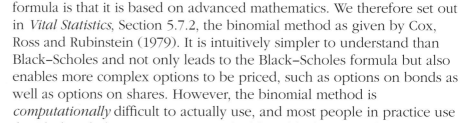

One problem in explaining the derivation of the Black–Scholes valuation formula is that it is based on advanced mathematics. We therefore set out in *Vital Statistics*, Section 5.7.2, the binomial method as given by Cox, Ross and Rubinstein (1979). It is intuitively simpler to understand than Black–Scholes and not only leads to the Black–Scholes formula but also enables more complex options to be priced, such as options on bonds as well as options on shares. However, the binomial method is *computationally* difficult to actually use, and most people in practice use the Black–Scholes equation. It may *look* horrible, but it can be programmed into a spreadsheet with little difficulty – though with considerable care, because it is easy to get wrong!

The Black–Scholes formula

In *Vital Statistics*, Section 5.7.2, we derive a value for a European call option on a share using the binomial method. The main difference between this approach and the Black–Scholes approach is that the binomial method looks at what happens to the call option price over *discrete* elements of time whereas the Black–Scholes model is in *continuous* time (those of you with a penchant for mathematics will realise that this assumption allows the use of calculus techniques). However, the two models – Cox, Ross and Rubinstein binomial and Black–Scholes – can be reconciled. It can be shown (but not here!) that, if we increase the number of intervals to infinity, the binomial model call value can be directly expressed by the Black–Scholes formula.

The Black–Scholes equation is given below. In all honesty, it does not look very friendly, but we will be concentrating on what are the constituent variables rather than the abstruse mathematics; it is clearly important to have some understanding of what factors affect option value, but we can rely on our computers to do the actual calculation for us.

So, taking a deep breath, have a look at the Black–Scholes call pricing equation:

$$C = SN(x) - Ke^{-rt}N(x - \sigma\sqrt{t})$$

where $x = [\ln(S/K) + (r + \sigma^2/2)t]/\sigma\sqrt{t}$, and ln is the natural logarithm function.

The meanings of the symbols are:

C = call option price

S = the current price of the share

K = the exercise or strike price

t = the time to expiry (in years)

r = the continuously compounded interest rate

σ = the volatility of the share price as measured by standard deviation (per annum)

The continuously compounded interest rate is obtained directly from the annual interest rate by the formula:

$$r = \ln(1 + \text{annual interest rate } \%/100)$$

The only additional form of notation is that of $N(x)$ which is the cumulative normal distribution function and for which tables are widely available. In practice, nowadays anyone using a spreadsheet package can construct a formula to calculate $N(x)$, and thus need only enter the values for the parameters for S, K, t, r and σ, and the computer will do the rest. This is demonstrated in the option valuation software on the B821 CD-ROM. So far, you have used this software as a 'black box', that is, not really knowing what was behind it. Slowly, but steadily, we are now disentangling the internal workings of that 'black box' for you.

In the software you will notice there is a label not considered by the Black–Scholes equation. This parameter [*Div Yld (%)*] helps to estimate the price of a European option on shares with known dividends. We will discuss why this is important later on. For the time being, consider that this innovation was introduced by Robert Merton and involved replacing S by Se^{-qt} in the Black–Scholes equation. In plain words, Merton substituted the strike price (*S*) for the product of the strike price (*S*) times an estimate of the average dividend yield rate (*q*) – per annum.

Hence, your option valuation model estimates the Merton equation. You can make the dividend yield rate equal to zero and then get the valuation of the Black–Scholes model in the software. Alternatively, you can use the share option valuation spreadsheet (EQOP). The Merton equation can be readily applied to value currency options; the option valuation software does this through 'create currency option'. Alternatively, you can use the Garman-Kohlhagen model to value currency options through the CURROP spreadsheet.

Warning! Rounding difference.

Whichever computational alternative you use, bear in mind that the software usually has a difference with the spreadsheet estimates at the second or third decimal level. For our purposes, this is trivial. But you will understand that wouldn't be the case in a real life situation.

Let us move on, as our purpose in this sub-section is to look at what factors are involved in determining the option value, and why they are important.

What are the important variables?

S – K, the difference between the current price and the exercise price

This is obviously going to be important. For example, if the strike price is much higher than the current price (out-of-the-money) then the likelihood of the option being exercised is small, and so is its value. Vice versa, if K < S (in-the-money) then the option is *already* worth money if exercised, and the lower K is, the higher that intrinsic value.

σ, the volatility

Think back to Activity 4.2, with companies Hi and Lo.

If the share price jumps around a lot – is very volatile – then the chances of S being much higher or lower at expiry than now is relatively high. But if we hold an option we can take benefit if it ends up that S > K but are not concerned if S < K, in which case we just let the option expire. So for option prices, volatility is *good*, because we are protected from the downside.

t, the time to expiry

The longer the option has to run, the greater the chance that the price will end up above the exercise price, so as *t* gets longer, the option value goes higher (everything else being equal).

As you might remember, this is the same as proposition 2 in Section 4. You might also remember that proposition 2 need not hold for European options on shares which paid a dividend. This would mean that, in principle, the Black–Scholes model would be good to price all commodity options except for those on shares. But wait, this can't be the right stuff for a Nobel Prize, can it? Enter Robert Merton, to the rescue!

The Nobel Prize for Economics was awarded to Myron Scholes (jointly with Robert Merton) in 1997 for his work on options. Sadly, Fischer Black died in 1995, before the Nobel Committee decided to present the Prize, which cannot be awarded posthumously. Robert Merton died in the Spring of 2000.

What Merton did was modify the Black–Scholes equation making it easier to price share options near the date companies announce their dividends. How? Very simple, by taking the idea behind the Gordon model (see 5.3.1. in *Vital Statistics*), which simply put says that: dividends are expected to grow at a constant rate of growth each year. The parameter *q*, therefore, is an estimate of the annual compounded dividend yield rate and provides a way to value European options on shares while complying with proposition 2.

r, the risk-free interest rate

This is involved because the Black–Scholes model takes into account the time value of money, so the higher the interest rate, the higher the option value.

Bearing in mind the linkage between call and put options – remember Proposition 5: Put–call parity – it is not surprising that the same factors affect the value of put options, though for the latter an out-of-the-money option is where K is *less* than S.

If this is not clear to you, look back at Figure 3.1 and your answer to Exercise 3.2.

The last 'conceptual' point you need to think about concerning the Black–Scholes model is: what is the key premise underlying the formula? While the mathematics is fairly horrendous, the concept is straightforward. In essence the idea is that at any instant, the profit or loss of holding an option for small changes in S (i.e. ΔC for ΔS) can be reproduced *exactly* by an equivalent portfolio consisting of a suitable number of the underlying shares and cash. 'All' one then has to do is ascertain the constituent proportions of that instantaneous portfolio and then double-integrate over t and S – simple! For a practising mathematician, at least; but the rest of us can at least reasonably expect to follow the process once it has been derived by those eligible for the Nobel Prize.

Activity 5.1

Read about the binomial model in Section 5.7.2 of *Vital Statistics*. As said earlier in this section, this is an alternative option valuation model, but one less easy to use and thus less popular. It is useful, however, for you to see that the problem can be attacked from another viewpoint – and that the final result ends up converging on that given by Black–Scholes anyway. Even if you actually use the Black–Scholes model, the ideas behind the binomial method can prove helpful in thinking about options and their evaluation.

The Black–Scholes formula is also useful in developing hedging strategies. The binomial model in *Vital Statistics* is based on the principle that we can duplicate the buying of a call option by taking a position in the underlying share *and* borrowing. In fact, N(x) in the Black–Scholes formula is the *number of shares* to buy in the duplicated position, so that SN(x) is the amount to be invested in shares, while $Ke^{-rt}N(x - \sigma\sqrt{t})$ is the *amount to be borrowed*. In order for the shares and borrowing position to mirror continually the call option position, the number of shares held will have to be altered every time the share price changes, but this will not require any change in total investment. In technical language, we define the call option **delta** (the number of shares per call) to be equal to N(x).

Thus, for every option held, the delta gives the number of shares which will enable the option position to be replicated. From the opposite perspective, for every share, the reciprocal of the delta tells you how many options will be needed to replicate the share position. An option's delta varies between 0 and 1 so, for example, an option with a delta of 0.2 implies that one share should be hedged with five of these options.

This duplication or hedging property via an option's delta is of great practical importance to anyone involved in options. For example, those holding shares can hedge their positions by writing call options and will be hedged continuously provided they adjust the number of shares every time the share price changes according to the delta. This type of hedging is known as **delta hedging** or **ratio hedging**. Indeed, the delta can also be defined as the number of pence change in an option price for a one penny change in the underlying share price. Notice that put options, which move in the opposite direction to share prices, becoming more valuable as share prices fall, will have negative deltas of between 0 and −1.

In Figure 5.1 we see the value of a call option for different current share prices which we first met in Figure 3.1. The curve represents the value of a call option for a particular exercise price, interest rate and volatility. For any particular share price (along the x-axis) we can 'read off' the option value.

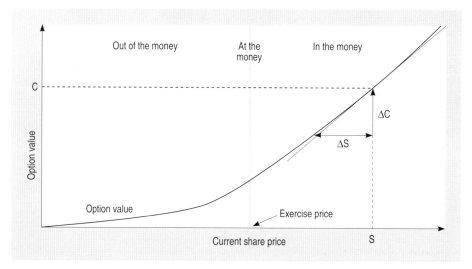

Figure 5.1 Value of a call option for different current share prices

So let us assume that at the moment the share price is S and the call value at S is C. The straight line just touching the curve at this point is the tangent to the call price curve for the point S on the x-axis. For small changes in the share value ΔS, there will be a small change in the option value ΔC such that

$$\Delta C = \Delta S \times \text{gradient of the tangent}$$

The gradient of the tangent is in fact the delta hedge ratio and is equal to N(x), although a proof of this is beyond the scope of this course. Since we now know that ΔC = ΔS × delta ratio, if one had 1/(delta ratio) options, the gain or loss would be exactly the same as if one held a share instead. So the two possibilities are equivalent.

Unfortunately, because the real option value line is a curve, the gradient (and therefore the delta hedge ratio) alters if S changes significantly, and one has to rebalance the holding to keep the hedge in place. So those practising delta hedging need to monitor the market almost continuously. The portfolio also needs to be large enough so that fairly small changes in the delta hedge ratio for each option contract can be translated into deals large enough to conduct cost-effectively in the market-place. In effect, only major players such as market-makers can really rely on using delta hedging.

BOX 5.1   WHEN IS A PORTFOLIO JUST A BIG OPTION?

This can be looked at in another way. Instead of starting with an option and replicating it, via the delta hedge ratio, by a package of shares and cash, why not *begin* with a portfolio of shares and cash and choose the proportions to make it act like an option? An important application of this is in portfolio insurance, where the amounts invested in shares and kept in cash are decided upon by calculating the delta ratio, so that a portfolio becomes transformed into call options with limited downside risk and unlimited upside potential.

A large number of major US funds have used this technique (to a greater or lesser extent) with the idea of giving up some of the benefits of higher share prices in exchange for having a minimum level below which the value of their funds could not fall. In the event, the very wide use of the technique caused it to be discredited in the crash of October 1987, since the rebalancing of shares and cash was done via the futures markets which became mis-priced relative to shares.

However, more recent analysis of the 1987 crash, perhaps with the objectivity of passing time, has largely exonerated the use of derivatives in the debacle. At worst, they may have hastened what was probably inevitable; nevertheless, for individual funds the protection gained was less than expected because the speed of the fall meant that the necessary 'rebalancing' of the 'insurance' was not possible.

It should be noted that the method described in Box 5.1, indeed any form of delta hedging, requires constant monitoring and frequent adjustment of the position. This is possible for market professionals but is not what most users of options for risk management would regard as a useful method. A typical corporate user will want to acquire a hedge against a particular risk and then be able to 'forget' about it until the deal matures. Nevertheless, it is useful to know that delta hedging is 'out there' as it helps explain why banks and other financial institutions are able to provide any sort of option requested by their customers – at a price! Even if there is no possible counterparty, the bank can 'create' the option by using delta hedging techniques.

Before we leave the Black–Scholes formula for a call option, we note an important point about the four parameters needed to value the call. Three of them (share-exercise price, time to expiry and interest rate) are the same for all market traders. Only the volatility value can be argued about.

What is *needed* is the volatility estimate for the period to expiry of the option. What is *used* is a historical measure of volatility, measured by standard deviation, for the past six days, six weeks, six months or a year. Each period used will give a different volatility estimate and hence a different call option value. Aczel (1987) gives a summary of these and other estimation methods.

There is nothing special about these periods. It is just an educated guess as to which past period will give the best estimate of future volatility.

Alternatively, what can be done is to input the market price of the option into the Black–Scholes formula and work out the **implied volatility** – that is, the volatility which gives the call value equal to the market price. Then, according to the investor's view on future volatility, the option can be seen as 'cheap' or 'dear'. The more volatile an asset, the more

The option valuation software can help you find implied volatility. Try it for each of the combinations in Table 4.2.

expensive are call or put options on the asset, just as the more likely your house is to burn down, the more expensive the insurance is. This gives traders a whole new perspective to investing in options since money can be made or lost, not just from price movements, but from changes in volatility. Holders of options will make money if markets are volatile, writers of options will lose. Indeed, many people use options as a means of taking a view on volatility – if they expect a market crash, they will buy put options. They will not hold the put options to expiry: before the volatility element will have disappeared from the option price, they will cash in after the market fall, making money both from the price fall and the volatility increase. To see the latter point, think of insurance premiums: the higher the risk the higher the premium. Volatility speculators bought when volatility was low, so the premium was (relatively) low; when the market falls they sell on their options, but now the new, higher volatility is included in the premiums they charge.

To conclude this brief look at the Black–Scholes model, let us consider a worked example. In this example, the parameters are as follows:

S = 400p

K = 350p

$t = {}^4\!/_{12}$ or 0.3333 (in years) or 120 days

$r = \ln(1.05)$ since the interest rate is 5%

σ = 30%

If you access the option valuation software on the B821 disk and put the five parameters from the share example as follows:

Volatility: 30.0

Current price: 400.0

Strike price: 350.0

Interest Rate: 5.0

Dividend Yield: 0

Maturity: 120

and look at the resulting call/put prices you will see:

Call option price: 62.4397 (or 15.6099% of S)

Put option price: 6.7334 (or 1.6833% of S)

Notice how the software estimates whole days rather than fractions of a year. Actually, 199.988 days is equivalent to 4/12 of a financial year. To see the importance of this difference, look how the premium value changes to 62.5489 for the call and 6.7955 for the put when Maturity changes to 121 days.

Alternatively, if you access the option valuation EQOP model on the CD-ROM and put in the five parameters from the share example as follows:

Domestic interest rate: 5.00%

Volatility: 30.00%

Maturity: 0.3333

Current price: 400.00

Exercise price: 350.00

and looking at the resulting call/put prices you will see:

Call option price: 62.5119 which is 15.6280% of S.

Put option price: 6.8663 which is 1.7166% of S.

We thus have a value of 62.5p for the call option.

Exercise 5.1 _____

Use the option valuation software or the equity option calculation spreadsheet EQOP to value a call option on a share priced at 100p with an exercise price of 75p, an interest rate of 10%, a volatility of 30% and a time to expiry of 2 months.

5.2 CURRENCY OPTIONS

We now turn to the particular case of **currency options**, which are frequently used in treasury management. To take a specific example, the *Financial Times* gave the following table for prices at the close of business on 11 November 1997, when the spot price was £/$1.6870.

Table 5.1

Philadelphia Stock Exchange £/$ options

£31,250 (cents per £1)

Exercise price	Calls			Puts		
	Nov '97	Dec '97	Jan '98	Nov '97	Dec '97	Jan '98
1.680	1.83	2.70	3.42	0.28	1.41	2.38
1.690	1.11	2.17	2.89	0.56	1.84	2.80
1.700	0.60	1.64	2.51	1.06	2.37	3.35

The option valuation software can help you find implied volatility. Try it for each of the combinations in Table 5.1.

Table 5.1 is very similar to Table 4.2 for share options, so we only need to comment briefly on the above table. The prices quoted are those on the Philadelphia Stock Exchange, the largest currency options market in the world. The expiry dates for the options are around the middle of each month (more exactly on the Friday before the third Wednesday of the month). The prices quoted are in US cents so that, for example, an investor pays 2.17 cents to have the right (but not the obligation) to buy £1 for $1.690 (the exercise price) up to the December expiry date. The contract size is £31,250, so all dealings must be for multiples of this amount.

Valuing currency options

A straightforward modification of the Black–Scholes formula has been developed for currency options by Garman and Kohlhagen (1983) and this is generally accepted by traders as giving the 'fair value' of these options. Even if it does not always fit exactly, it gives the market standard and is therefore valuable to have. The Garman–Kohlhagen formula is:

$$C = e^{-r_F t} S N(x) - K e^{-r_D t} N(x - \sigma\sqrt{t})$$
$$x = [\ln(S/K) + (r_D - r_F + \sigma^2/2)t]/\sigma\sqrt{t}$$

The meanings of the symbols are:

C = call option price

S = the spot price of the currency

K = the exercise price

t = the time to expiry

r_D = 1 + the continuously compounded domestic interest rate

r_F = 1 + the continuously compounded foreign interest rate

σ = the exchange rate volatility or standard deviation as a percentage (per annum).

Use the 'Single Currency Option' screen in the option valuation model.

As noted before, the Merton model can also be used to value currency options. This is possible when considering that a foreign currency is analogous to a share paying a known dividend yield: the owner of foreign currency receives a 'dividend yield' equal to the risk-free rate in that country, r_F. We can now use either formula to value the December $1.690 option in Table 5.1. The parameters are as follows:

S = $1.687/£1

K = $1.690/£1

t = 1.25/12 or 0.104 years (37.5 days)

r_F = ln(1.05625) (since the interest rate is 5.625%)

r_D = ln(1.075) (since the interest rate is 7.5%)

σ = 10% (a rough figure based on the average at the time).

If you now access the currency option valuation model in the B821 computer software, and input the six parameters in the requested format:

Domestic interest rate: 7.5%

Foreign interest rate: 5.625%

Volatility: 10.00%

Maturity: 0.104

Spot price: 1.687

Exercise price: 1.690

you will get the following values for the options:

CALL/PUT ON FX

Call option price 0.0216 which is 1.2818% of S.

Put option price: 0.0215 which is 1.2765% of S.

So, the 'fair' value according to the Garman–Kohlhagen model or the Merton equation is 2.16 cents, not far from the quoted price of 2.17 cents in Table 5.1. In fact a volatility of 10.05 would give exactly 2.17 cents.

Exercise 5.2

Use the computer software to value the Jan '98 1.700 sterling put option with the same volatility and interest rate assumptions as in the previous example.

5.3 EXAMPLES AND CASES USING OPTIONS

An example of the use of currency options

Dorcas Spencer, the Production Director of Francis & Co., is very pleased to hear that the company could well receive a large order from one of its US customers. She understands that Francis are quoting in competition with other companies, so that they are not absolutely sure of getting the order, but they still appear to have a good chance. The order is for $2.5 million, so the UK supplier has to take the currency risk and, in the light of the way that the exchange rate has been moving up and down, this worries her. She puts the facts to Jan Parkinson, the Finance Director, and after doing some homework they have a meeting on 1 June 1998 to decide what to do. Jan starts by saying:

> As I understand it, if we get the order we shall be paid in the middle of August, so that what concerns us is what the spot rate will then be. The current rate is $1.677/£1 and I think it realistic to take an upper rate of $1.75/£1 in August and a lower rate of $1.60/£1 – barring serious changes the rate should lie somewhere in that range. We also need to look at where we shall be if we do get the order and where we shall be if we don't, so there are four cases to consider and I have summarised the outcomes in Table 5.2.

Table 5.2 Possible receipts from $2.5 million order				
	If we get the order		**If we do not get the order**	
Spot $/£ rate in August	$1.75	$1.60	$1.75	$1.60
	£000	£000	£000	£000
No hedge taken	1,429	1,563	0	0
Forward sale	1,512	1,512	83	−51
Option bought	1,474	1,544	46	−18

There are basically three courses of action we can take, as set out in the table:

(i) We can just take pot luck, and take no hedging action at all, so that we sell the dollars in August at the then spot rate. If, for instance, the rate has risen to $1.75/£ then what we would get is $2,500,000/1.75 = £1,429,000. If we do get the order, the danger we run is that the rate rises by then; if we do not get the order we run no risk under this strategy.

(ii) We can sell the dollars forward, and I have checked with our bank that the mid-August rate is $1.6539/£1. If we get paid in mid-August then we would get $2,500,000/1.6539 = £1,512,000 whatever the spot rate is then. We run a risk, however, if we do not get the order as we would then need to buy the dollars in to deliver them: thus, if the rate falls to $1.60/£1, we would end up with £1,512,000 less £1,563,000 or a loss of £51,000.

(iii) Our third strategy is to buy options on the Philadelphia Exchange. I have found that we can get call options with an exercise price of $1.675 at 2.03 cents for August. My calculations are that we would need to get options on $2,500,000/1.675 = £1,492,537 (I have not taken into account the need to buy an exact number of contracts). This would cost us £1,492,537 × 2.03/(1.677 × 100) = £18,000.

The premium is paid at the start of the contract and so the current spot rate of 1.677 is used to calculate the sterling cost of the premium.

If we do get the contract, we still sell the dollars on the open market and if the August spot rate is below $1.675/£1, the call option lapses and we get the receipts less our initial cost of £18,000. If the August spot rate is above $1.675/£1, then we get, after the initial cost, £1,474,000, regardless of the then spot rate, since the loss in the receipt due to the higher spot rate is exactly matched by the gain on the call option.

If we do not get the contract, the maximum we can lose is our initial investment of £18,000, which is less than the £51,000 we lose on selling forward if the rate is $1.60/£1 (and the loss on forward sale can be even higher).

Our decision really depends on how certain we are to get the order. If we are absolutely certain, the best bet is to sell forward; if we are not, we should take the option route.

Where to use currency options

The situations where currency options have real advantages in hedging are well set out in Ross *et al.* (1987). They can be summarised as follows:

- The loss to the hedger is limited to the premium paid, but the profit opportunity is unlimited. Options are thus a good way of limiting downside risk.

- They are a good way of hedging contingent cash flows, which may or may not occur.

- They provide a range of different ways of hedging, through the availability of different striking prices, unlike forward and futures markets which deal at a single price.

- They may not require daily margins (although Philadelphia options do) or a bank line of credit, as the forward market does.

So far, our discussion has proceeded as if traded options (and particularly those in the Philadelphia exchange), were the main market for currency options. However, this is not the case. The growth in the market for currency options known as **over-the-counter** or **OTC** currency **options** was the one which gave rise to the market for traded options. It is true that Philadelphia is a major market for traded options but there are other organised markets for currency derivatives such as the ones in Chicago or in many local financial centres.

OTC options are offered by banks to companies on a tailor-made basis, to suit each company's particular situation. Traded options have the advantage over OTC options of being readily marketable, and often can be cheaper (per currency unit). Some of the ways in which OTC options have advantages are that they are available:

- in many more currencies than traded options, which are only offered in the main currencies;

- for longer maturity than traded options;

- for maturity and value that match the exact requirements of the company (i.e. are tailored to the precise financial requirements of the buyer).

In comparison to traded options, OTC options do not require a daily margin to be maintained. However, in some instances they might modify the company's credit standing with its banks. Thus, the OTC market offers additional services besides traded option markets.

To conclude our very brief look at the whole field of options and the other derivatives you have met in this and its preceding unit, you will read a pair of recent articles describing what is going on at the fringe in this type of financial engineering.

Activity 5.2

Please read Tufano's article 'How financial engineering can advance corporate strategy' in the Course Reader.

It consists of four cases which show clever and/or innovative uses of derivatives; note that this encompasses more than the options group we have been considering in this section, so please read the article in the context of this block as a whole.

Activity 5.3

In similar vein, please read Brady's article 'New ways with derivatives' in the Course Reader.

There is some overlap with the preceding reading, but it is not significant. This second paper should broaden still further your appreciation of the applicability of the ideas you have been studying over these three units.

SUMMARY

Valuing options was the topic of this last book in the Financial Risk Management block. You were introduced to the Black–Scholes formula for share options and the Garman–Kohlhagen variant for currency options. Both formulae look quite horrible but are, actually, very amenable to programming into a spreadsheet. You have an option valuation software on your B821 disk (as well as the EQOP and CURROP spreadsheets), which you can use for valuing simple transactions with share and currency options. You also took a brief look, via *Vital Statistics*, at the binomial model.

The key things to remember from this valuation section are the range of variables that can affect the value of an option, and the idea of instantaneous equivalence between an option and holding a proportion of the underlying instrument – the idea of delta-hedging. Together, these give the crucial concept behind Black–Scholes methods of valuation. All the rest of the genuinely complex mathematics is unnecessary for a general manager's understanding of financial options. However, do remember there are derivatives on many other markets such as stock indexes, gold, oil, bonds and many agricultural commodities.

We concluded the section by looking at some of the ways options can be and are used in the world of business. They are already a very useful group of instruments for risk management, and as the range increases – and as understanding grows – they will assume an increasing significance in any system of financial risk control.

6 RISK AND POLICY

Over the last three units you have looked at financial risk of many types, together with some representative examples of the products available for managing such risk. It is now time to move from the essentially tactical level of operational risk management to consider the strategic framework which should inform, and within which, such activity can efficiently be carried out.

In the first sub-section we will look at the evidence for risk management shown in four companies' Annual Reports; over the block you have learnt about techniques and products for managing risk, especially financial risk. It seems reasonable to show to you that this is not merely academic thumb-twiddling or of interest only to banking 'rocket scientists', but is a serious concern for senior managers in organisations of all types.

BOX 6.1   WHY BANKERS READ TSIOLKOVSKY

Over the last 20 years (or so) the key people in banks responsible for the development of many of the risk management products you have been learning about, such as options and swaps, have come to be referred to as 'the rocket scientists'. Usually this is thought to be just a slang term attached to them simply because it gave an impression of high intelligence. Actually the term was applied because originally it was precisely true!

In the late 1970s the major American investment banks on Wall Street realised that they needed an injection of mathematical ability to make best use of the new theories reaching 'the street' – remember that Black and Scholes published their classic paper on option valuation in 1973.

Where could the banks find a sufficient source of ready-made applied mathematicians? Fortunately for Wall Street, their need coincided with a considerable 'downsizing' in NASA's fortunes following the end of the Apollo Program. So the banks' recruiters made a bee-line for the heat and humidity of Houston to buy themselves some PhDs. And thus their technical departments really did come to be stuffed with rocket scientists!

So why Tsiolkovsky? Because he was the Russian visionary (1857–1935) regarded as the 'Father of Rocketry', and most of the new bankers liked to pretend to themselves that they were only pocketing the inflated New York pay-packets while waiting for the 1980s' Mars Program that was sure to be announced ...

After seeing practical examples from other businesses, we will discuss some of the general points you ought to consider if (and when) you become responsible for prescribing risk policy for your own organisation. We then conclude this section by analysing a video case study which looks at risk management at TNT, a major international courier business.

6.1   EXAMPLES OF RISK POLICY

In Audio programme 4, which you listened to for Unit 7, you heard about the attitude to risk management at Bass plc and the BBC. That discussion looked at risk in the broad sense needed to understand 'risk mapping'. Here we will investigate more precisely the *financial* risk policy of some businesses as set out in their Annual Reports. The companies we will consider are Boots and Blue Circle; to prove that one should be serious about risk policy even if the organisation's name does not begin with 'B', we will also consider Carlton Communications. In each case the information has been extracted from the 1997 Annual Report, and the intent was to pick out the parts that had a direct relevance to topics discussed in this block. In case you would like to see the extracts in their original context, page numbers are given and these refer to the original printed report.

You can read through the extracts quickly, as the aim is simply to provide evidence for how a variety of companies make policy decisions concerning risk management; there are no deep theoretical points requiring intricate analysis. Nevertheless, it is useful and informative to see what organisations actually do about the matter.

Boots

In the Chairman's statement (p. 3), Sir Michael Angus comments on the Millennium and EMU; the former echoes another aspect of a concern described by Paul Hopkin in Audio 4 and the latter compares the 'millennium effect' with that of EMU, which will be much more fundamental in the long run.

> **The Millennium** We fully recognise the importance of putting in place the business systems for this event. We estimate that some 300 man years of effort are required to amend or update our systems across the group. We believe this may be less than for some comparable organisations since we have a progressive plan of systems enhancement and replacement and therefore have been working on the programme for some considerable time.
>
> Preparation for the Millennium is not, however, simply an information technology issue. We have designated managers in each of our businesses to handle this, in close co-operation with our suppliers of products and services. Obviously we seek to ensure that our normal business operations are not disrupted as systems changes are made.
>
> **European Monetary Union** This is a serious issue for retailers, who will be at the front line in managing the transition for consumers if and when it comes. We are acutely conscious of the potential impact and we have a team examining the implications for our business. The scale of cost for all retailers would be considerably greater than that relating to the Millennium.

The Financial Review gives a clear statement about risk policy (p. 8):

> **Treasury control policy** We have clear principles covering all major aspects of treasury policy. These aim to benefit long term shareholders. Strict guidelines for cash investments apply worldwide, and investments

are made only in high quality bank deposits and other liquid instruments.

Controls are in place which seek to prevent fraud and other unauthorised transactions and minimise counterparty risk. There are regular reviews by the group's internal audit staff.

Interest rate policy We continue to believe that hedging the impact of short term movements in interest rates does not increase the worth of the company and that long term shareholders do not ascribe value to the reduction in earnings volatility resulting from such hedging.

In common with other UK retailers, the group has significant liabilities through its obligations to pay rents under property leases, the implicit interest rate on which can be considered to be fixed.

Some years ago the board adopted a strategy of regular long term interest rate swaps in order to change the balance between fixed and floating rate debt. This activity is strictly controlled and monitored, each swap being authorised by the group finance director.

At the year end the total volume of interest rate swaps on leases was £675 million, with £325 million being undertaken during this year. All of these swaps were done with a maturity of ten years to match the long term nature of the underlying property leases. [...]

Currency exposure policy Modest sales and purchases are made in a range of currencies, but it is not considered that hedging them into sterling adds value.

The statement on corporate governance describes the board-level responsibility for internal financial control (p. 39):

Internal control

The directors are responsible for the group's system of internal financial control. These controls are established in order to safeguard the group's assets, maintain proper accounting records and ensure that financial information used within the business or published is reliable.

The company has an established framework of internal financial controls, the key elements of which are as follows:

- Members of the board have responsibility for monitoring the conduct and operations of individual businesses within the group. This includes the review and approval of business strategies and plans and the setting of key business performance targets. The group has a formal and comprehensive process for the determination of business strategies and this process is co-ordinated and monitored by group headquarters. The executive management responsible for each business are accountable for the conduct and performance of their business within the agreed strategies.

- Business plans provide a framework from which performance commitments have been agreed by group headquarters with each business. These commitments incorporate financial and strategic targets against which business performance is monitored. This monitoring includes the examination of and changes to rolling annual and half year forecasts and monthly measurement of actual achievement against key performance targets and budgets. These results are consolidated, appraised and communicated to the board.

- The company has clear requirements for the approval and control of expenditure. Investment decisions involving capital or revenue expenditure are subject to formal detailed appraisal and review according to approval levels set by the board. Significant expenditure of this nature requires approval by a director or the board. Performance reviews are undertaken by the businesses on completion of investments. Operating expenditure is controlled within each business with approval levels for such expenditure being determined by the individual businesses.

● There are clear procedures for monitoring the system of internal financial control. The audit committee meets at least three times a year [...] . It receives reports from the internal audit function on the results of work carried out under an annual risk focused internal audit plan and from the external auditors. It also requests the attendance of business management, as required, to report on controls relating to specific business activity. Internal audit also facilitate an annual process whereby businesses provide certified statements of compliance with internal financial controls, which are supported by summaries of key control activities and an assessment of significant risks, controls and resulting exposures.

On behalf of the board, the audit committee has reviewed the effectiveness of the system of internal financial control. The review revealed that reasonable steps have been taken to ensure that there is a system of internal financial control which is appropriate for a group of this size and diversity. It should be recognised that any such system can, however, provide only reasonable, and not absolute, assurance against material misstatement or loss.

'Accounting Policies' lays out the treatment of foreign currencies (p. 54); note that the company uses an average rate basis for converting overseas results. This is a common practice, but so is using a year-end rate; to an auditor either is acceptable as long as the practice is applied consistently.

Foreign currencies

The results and cash flows of overseas subsidiaries are translated into sterling on an average exchange rate basis, weighted by the actual results of each month. Assets and liabilities including currency swaps are translated into sterling at the rates of exchange ruling at the balance sheet date.

Exchange differences arising from the translation of the results and net assets of overseas subsidiaries, less offsetting exchange differences on foreign currency borrowings and currency swaps hedging those assets, are dealt with through reserves.

All other exchange differences are dealt with in the profit and loss account.

The cost of the parent company investment in shares in overseas subsidiaries is stated at the rate of exchange in force at the date each investment was made.

The last reference we will make concerns swaps, both single-currency and cross-currency (p. 68). Note that Boots still uses the terms 'interest rate' and 'currency' respectively. We quote only the two notes referring to swaps, the borrowings total being less relevant to this discussion.

Borrowings

e The group has a number of US dollar currency swaps, which are equivalent to borrowing US dollars and depositing sterling for a fixed period. Following the disposal of Boots Pharmaceuticals on 31st March 1995, the group put in place a series of matching swaps, which are equivalent to depositing US dollars and borrowing sterling. The net liability shown above represents the effect of translating the above transactions into sterling at the year end exchange rate.

f The group has a number of interest rate swap agreements which convert fixed rate liabilities to floating rate. The fixed rate commitments effectively converted are £85m of the 10.125% bond, £675m of operating leases and £95m referred to in note a above.

Remember from Unit 7 that we prefer to use the more modern terms single- and cross-currency swaps because they describe the transactions more clearly. But at the time of writing the older terminology is still much used.

Blue Circle

The Group Finance Director gives a quite detailed description of the risk management policy in his Review (pp. 8–9).

> **Risk management** The main financial risks for the Group relate to exchange rates and interest rates.
>
> The Group does not hedge book profit translation exposures to exchange rate changes, but its policy is to hedge foreign exchange transactions either in the forward market or by using options. The Group's profit before tax in 1997 would have been £20 million higher translated at average 1996 exchange rates.
>
> Details of the currencies of borrowings and net assets are shown on page 59. As can be seen, borrowings have been made in the same currencies as the Group's continental European and North American assets and these, together with currency swaps, reduce balance sheet exposure to exchange rate changes. A similar approach is not always taken to assets elsewhere in the world because of the high cost of borrowing in matching currencies.
>
> The Group's cash and short-term investments of £363.5 million are mainly held in the UK in sterling in high quality short-term assets. Credit limits are set for all counterparties. There is no material amount of overseas cash subject to restricted repatriation because of foreign exchange regulations.
>
> Interest rate exposure on borrowings and deposits is managed with the help of interest rate swaps. The proportions of fixed and floating rate borrowings held by the Group vary according to the interest rate cycle; at the end of 1997 some 45 per cent of gross borrowings including currency swaps was at fixed rates. With no changes to the borrowings and hedges, a 1 per cent interest rate rise in the currencies in which the Group has borrowings and/or earns interest would increase profits before tax by 0.4 per cent. The Group also manages its borrowings maturity profile; some 41 per cent of its gross borrowings at the end of 1997 had a maturity of more than 5 years. Commercial paper debts of £187.1 million shown in the Group Balance Sheet as maturing in under one year have back-up facilities with a maturity of 2 years.
>
> **Treasury Department** In addition to risk management, Treasury operates as a service department giving funding and general advice. It does not undertake transactions which are speculative or unrelated to the Group's trading activities. Its policies are subject to Board review and its activities to internal audit.

Exercise 6.1 _____

Boots does not make a practice of hedging whereas Blue Circle does for what we have defined as 'transaction exposure'. Can you suggest a reason for the difference in policy?

BOX 6.2   WHEN IS A HEDGE NOT A HEDGE?

In Exercise 6.1, there is an implication that neither Boots nor Blue Circle hedge 'translation risk'. Does this mean that businesses see such risk as irrelevant, in which case why did we include it in Unit 8? In fact this is not the case, the difference being what one considers as 'hedging action'. The Annual Reports take, quite understandably, an 'accounting' view, by which we mean that they include only specific, extra transactions undertaken solely for the purpose of hedging; in this block, on the other hand, we have taken a rather more 'operational' approach.

We therefore include as 'hedging' any activity which reduces risk by altering or varying transactions which would have been needed anyway. The clearest example of this would be 'matching' of foreign assets and liabilities, where funding which would have been required anyway is actually raised in a currency 'matching' that of the fixed assets. We would regard that as 'hedging' because it avoids translation exposure even before it crystallises. From the Annual Report point of view this is not 'hedging', since the risk never arose. We include avoidance, the accountants do not.

There is an explicit indication of this difference on p. 59 of the Blue Circle Annual Report:

'There were no significant unmatched foreign currency assets and liabilities. Matched assets and liabilities are those that generate no gain or loss in the profit and loss account, either because they are denominated in the same currency as the Group operation to which they belong or because they qualify under SSAP 20 as a foreign currency borrowing providing a hedge against a foreign equity investment.'

On p. 34 Blue Circle discloses in its 'Report of Directors' detail of its control policy, and we reproduce the relevant section:

Control environment

There is a clearly defined organisational structure within which individual responsibilities are identified in relation to internal financial controls. The structure is complemented by policies laid down in Group manuals and management is required to confirm that they operate the business in compliance with these policies. The policies include strict rules for the authorisation and approval of both revenue and capital expenditure.

Identification of business risk

The Group has reporting procedures that identify the major financial business risks within the Group. Policies and procedures have been laid down for the regular review and management of these risks. The Group's internal audit department undertakes regular reviews of the most significant areas of risk and ensures that key control objectives remain in place.

Information systems

There is a comprehensive budgeting system with a business plan approved by the Board in January of each year. Each month, management accounts containing actual and budget results and revised forecasts for the year are prepared and reported to the Board. These monthly management accounts analyse and explain variances against plan and report on key financial indicators.

Main control procedures

The Group has defined procedures and financial controls, including information system controls, to ensure the reporting of complete and accurate accounting information. These cover systems for obtaining authority for major transactions and for ensuring compliance with laws and regulations that have significant financial implications. Procedures are also in place to ensure that assets are subject to proper physical controls and that the organisation remains structured to ensure appropriate segregation of duties.

Monitoring

The monitoring of financial control procedures is achieved through management review by the responsible executive director reporting to the Board. These are supplemented by comprehensive reviews undertaken by the internal audit department on the controls in operation in each individual business. The internal audit department produces regular reports addressed to senior management that assess the impact of control issues and recommend appropriate actions.

What can one draw out of this extract? The emphasis here is on the identification of financial risks, and ensuring that systems are in place for tracking and controlling these risks as they pass through the organisation. Remember that this extract comes from a particularly 'formal' part of the Annual Report concerning the directors' responsibilities as stewards of the shareholders' investment; the 'managerial' aspect of risk management policy was described in the earlier extract from the Finance Director's statement. This is quite a pragmatic distinction, recognising that the board members as a whole are jointly responsible for control, but delegating actual management of the field to the finance director as representing the specialist department. This is appropriate, provided that the other directors know enough about the subject to ask appropriate questions and provide the necessary checks and balances for the finance director's fiefdom that they would naturally apply to all other aspects of the organisation.

As with Boots, the Accounting Policy states the rate policy for consolidating foreign results into the Group figures (p. 42):

4   Foreign currency

Profit and loss accounts of foreign entities in foreign currencies are translated into sterling at average rates for the year. Assets and liabilities denominated in foreign currencies are translated into sterling at the rates of exchange ruling at 31 December. Exchange differences arising on translation of net assets in overseas subsidiaries and related companies held at the beginning of the year, together with those differences resulting from the restatement of profits and losses from average to year-end rates, are taken to reserves.

Exchange differences arising on foreign currency borrowings raised to finance equity investments denominated in a foreign currency are taken to reserves on consolidation and offset against the exchange differences arising on those assets.

All other exchange differences are included in the profit and loss account.

Lastly, in the Note to the Accounts regarding 'Borrowings' it is shown that about one-third of the company's borrowings were subject to off-balance sheet cross-currency swaps, and that single-currency swaps were also used for interest rate management. The information is not quoted here as it is spread through the quite lengthy 'Borrowings' section. If you wish to read the source material, it is Note 17 on pp. 58–60.

Carlton Communications

As well as the usual comments regarding accounting policy (p. 36) and effect of swaps on borrowings (p. 50), Carlton gives as part of the Financial Director's review an exemplary description of its financial risk management (pp. 26–7):

Treasury

Objectives, policies and strategies

The most significant treasury exposures faced by Carlton are in relation to the ability to raise finance to support its activities, the management of interest rate and currency positions and the investment of surplus cash in high quality assets. Clear parameters have been established, including levels of authority, on the type and use of financial instruments to manage these exposures. Transactions are only undertaken if they relate to underlying exposures and cannot be viewed as speculative. Regular reports are provided to senior management and treasury operations are subject to periodic independent reviews and audits, both internal and external.

Financing

Carlton's policy is to finance itself long term with a mixture of equity and debt instruments with a range of maturities. Carlton has traditionally raised fixed rate debt from the US and European Capital Markets, as well as obtaining bank facilities from the UK Syndicated market. In accordance with this policy, Carlton raised £200 million of 10 year finance in May 1997 from the Sterling Eurobond market at a total cost of 7.90%.

At the year end Carlton had a committed £150m syndicated bank facility with a maturity of November 2001 provided by a group of high quality international banks. The purpose of the facility is to provide backstop liquidity; backing for Carlton's commercial paper programme; and the maintenance of a group of core relationship banks to support Carlton in its future activities.

Interest rate management

Carlton uses interest swaps, options and forward rate agreements to manage its interest rate exposures on its debt and cash positions.

In accordance with this policy, in January 1997, Carlton executed a series of interest rate swap contracts which have effectively reduced Carlton's interest rate exposure under the $150m Undated Exchangeable Capital Securities from 8% to 6.23% for the period to October 1998, saving $4.6m.

At the year end, and after taking account of interest rate swaps, the proportion of Carlton's borrowings at fixed rates was 76% and the proportion of cash at fixed rates was nil. Net interest receivable was £0.8m and a 1% increase in short term sterling and dollar interest rates based on the year end position would increase profits before tax by about £3.8m.

Borrowings are denominated in currencies that match Carlton's net assets as described below. At the year end, the fair value of borrowings and swap contracts exceeded their nominal value by £12.2m. The difference was primarily due to current interest rates being lower than those prevailing when part of the borrowing was raised.

Currency management

Carlton faces currency exposures on the translation of profits earned in overseas subsidiaries, primarily in the USA (profit translation exposure), and on trading transactions undertaken by its subsidiaries in foreign currencies (transactional exposure).

Carlton is also subject to currency exposures on the translation of the net assets of its overseas subsidiaries, primarily in the USA (balance sheet translation exposure).

Carlton does not usually hedge its profit translation exposures as these are an accounting rather than cash exposure. In addition, as Carlton accounts for currency profits using average exchange rates, there is a smoothing effect on short-term currency movements.

Carlton does hedge a proportion of its transactional exposures by taking out forward foreign exchange contracts of up to two years forward against its anticipated and known sales and purchases. The decision to hedge is influenced by the size of exposure; the certainty of it arising; the trading and market position of the company in which the exposure arises; and the current exchange rate.

At the year end Carlton had forward cover for 33% of the next year's anticipated and known transactional exposure. The year end spot value of these contracts was £0.4m above their book value, due to the strength of sterling.

Carlton's balance sheet translation exposure is managed by partially matching currency assets with currency borrowings. Details of the currencies of borrowings and net assets at the year end are illustrated on page 26 and these are not materially different from the average position in the year. Carlton's primary balance sheet translation exposure is against the dollar and it targets a 50% hedged position in the long run. At the year end Carlton's balance sheet translation exposure was 40% hedged.

During the year sterling strengthened against all the major currencies to which Carlton is exposed. The effect on profit translation was to reduce profits on a year on year basis by £6.6m, mainly due to the average dollar translation rate increasing from $1.55 to $1.63.

Currency exchange on trading transactions would also have had a negative impact on profits due to sterling strength, but this exposure is less significant. Exposure to the dollar is Carlton's largest single currency exposure and a movement against sterling by one cent, if maintained over the whole year, would affect reported profits by approximately £0.8m.

Investment of cash
Carlton operates strict investment guidelines with respect to surplus cash and the emphasis is on preservation of capital. Consequently investments with a maturity greater than one year must be rated AA or better and investments of less than one year must be rated A1 or P1 by the major credit rating agencies. There are also conservative limits for individual counterparties. During 1997 and at 30 September 1997 all cash was invested with maturities of less than one year.

It is worth noting that Carlton *does* regard 'matching' as hedging activity, which shows that the exact definition of what constitutes risk management is somewhat dependent on viewpoint. But the actions – netting, matching and so on – are similar across organisations even if they differ in how to categorise them for reporting purposes.

You should also note that Carlton is alone among the three companies looked at in stating clearly that it makes use of options (see the paragraph on 'Interest rate management'). This does not necessarily mean that Boots and Blue Circle make no use of option products, but at the present time an estimate that about one in three major companies use options would probably not be too wide of the mark. Except that we know *all* organisations buy some out-of-the-money options, but call it insurance!

Let us conclude the sub-section with an activity for you to investigate another organisation's statement of policy.

Activity 6.1 _____

Please find another Annual Report and see what that organisation says about its risk management policy. You may want to look at the accounts for your own organisation, or try searching the Internet for a business that interests you. On the B821 Web page we include links to Boots, Blue Circle and Carlton accounts so that you can see changes over time in attitude towards or scope of risk management using the examples you have just been reading about.

6.2 ELEMENTS OF POLICY-SETTING FOR RISK MANAGEMENT

At the beginning of this block we started this policy-level work by discussing the idea of a risk mapping for the organisation. As was said there, such an audit is essentially an information exercise which ought to enable better policy to be set by the board of directors (or equivalent). It is important to note that it is the whole board of directors which is referred to for policy-setting. Unfortunately it is too often the case that this devolves to being the finance director – a dangerous abrogation of joint responsibility.

As discussed in Unit 7, it is vital that the allocation of risk capacity be done on a holistic basis, considering the needs and opportunities of the complete organisation and not just of the finance function. It is often more difficult to assess the other risks of a business, or they are less obvious than those associated with the treasury operations, and so it requires discipline to keep in balance the time devoted to considering each of the various types of risk. For example, as you read in the Brady article in the previous section, 'oil companies spending vast amounts of time looking at interest rate management ... hundreds of times less important than the risk of a fall in the price of oil'. Given that most oil companies are inherently experienced at project appraisal and risk analysis, if they can make such a mistake it is clear that we are all in danger of falling into the same trap.

Clearly, policy-making is not only about allocation of risk capacity. It must also provide the structure of guidelines within which the organisation deals with risk items on a daily basis. It is not possible to generalise about what those guidelines should cover as it depends to such an extent on the nature of the aspect of operations under consideration.

However, there are some points that one would expect most such sets of guidelines to cover. These would include the following.

- the objectives of the sub-set of the organisation, and how they relate to the overall goals of the business
- 'typical' operations, i.e. the way most transactions or situations should be dealt with
- atypical but not particularly unusual events
- 'in case of emergency', i.e. catastrophic occurrences
- security procedures, e.g. dual signatures on external payments
- information reporting and performance measures

- the 'chain of command', i.e. who can take responsibility for what level of decision
- the boundaries within which line management can operate.

The first and last in the list are probably the most important elements for senior management to decide upon for themselves; they should be responsible for agreeing the others but can delegate the task of guideline construction to the line managers.

Clearly, this is a non-exhaustive list, and not all of the points will prove relevant in all situations. Nevertheless, a policy guideline which addressed each of the topics adequately for all aspects of the organisation would be a very reasonable starting point for good managerial control – a good grip on the business.

An example: the role of trustees in fund management

As mentioned in the foregoing, you cannot be too general about setting policy, but you *can* see analogies from particular examples.

Trusteeship and fund management are discussed again in Unit 10.

Let us now look at the way a board of trustees should go about setting up the investment guidelines for a pension or investment fund. This example is chosen because it is relevant to a finance course, but also because some – perhaps many – of you may later in your careers find yourself in such a trustee position; for example, for your own organisation's pension fund. And all research done to date shows that most trustees have little understanding of their responsibilities in this area – or the extent of their liability if it all goes wrong and they are shown to have been negligent in their duties.

First, the trustees need to be clear about the boundary between their role and that of the fund's investment manager(s), who can be taken as representing the professional 'line management' function. The trustees are responsible for policy, the fund manager for implementation, so the former should be setting:

- needs and aims
- investment guidelines
- measures of performance.

Examples of these are discussed in Unit 10. Taking the three areas in turn, the board as a whole, and the trustees as individuals, must take responsibility for defining the objectives of the fund in terms that can be used to advise the operational management of the fund. Thus the trustees should consider what should be the appropriate risk appetite for the fund, taking into account the 'profile' of the current and future beneficiaries. We hope that by now you are convinced that there is a link between risk and return; as a trustee, therefore, you need to assess what risk appetite is sensible so that the fund manager can try to maximise overall return in an acceptable way.

"We're all right as long as they think we're talking millions."

One practical way to go about this would be to base it on the demographics of the organisation, by which we mean: 'Is it an "old" or a "young" fund?' If the business is old but declining the fund probably has relatively few young, long-term contributors and many people near to or in retirement and should be more concerned about stability of income and values over the near term – the pre-privatisation British coal industry's pension fund would be a good example. Therefore, its trustees should be willing to forgo a certain amount of expected return in exchange for a stable flow of cash to beneficiaries.

At the other extreme, think about the fund for a small computer software company; it may well have no expected retirees for another 30 years, and an average age of under 25 for contributors/beneficiaries. The board for such a fund should be willing to accept a higher level of variability in short-term results in order to capture a better average return over the long term.

'Near term' here is a relative concept; a pension fund with all beneficiaries already retired will probably still be looking to a period of twenty to thirty years.

The board can certainly demand expert assistance, for example from the fund's actuary, in assessing where on the 'age scale' the fund resides, but ultimately it is the trustees' duty to decide upon an acceptable level of risk for the pension fund. They should also consider any constraints that need to be placed upon the fund manager; for example, is it an 'ethical' fund, or are the firm's competitors to be excluded, and so on. In each case it is the board's responsibility to maintain the balance between 'good citizenship' and its legal duty to maximise the fund's value to beneficiaries. If the investment vehicle has been set up and sold with a specific nature in mind, for example 'environmentally friendly', then the trustees have a mandate to forgo some element of diversification to meet the stated requirement, but can the same be said for an 'ordinary' company pension fund?

Having ascertained the risk capacity for the fund, the board should also consider policy concerning the balance between income and growth, and for cash-flow management. In practice such aspects are usually predicated upon the decision of the level of risk, together with the data which informed it.

Again, you will see how this is done in Unit 10.

Activity 6.2

Think about your own organisation, and estimate the age profile of the employees. How long should the planning horizon for its pension fund (if it has one) be? What do you think its level of risk should be?

So now we have 'aims and objectives', but the board's work is not over yet. It needs to set policy guidelines within which the fund manager can work, giving sufficient indication as to 'acceptability' without restricting flexibility unduly. With due regard to the tenets of portfolio theory, it is more reasonable to expect people with investment expertise to be able to make a contribution by economic analysis of markets and products than by regular stock-picking. In essence, what is being implied is that EMH is less true across geographic, market and product boundaries than within, say, a particular equity market. If the trustees really believe in global strong-form EMH, then they hardly need an investment manager at all, simply a passive fund manager aiming to track a relevant index – a 'beta-watcher' – and a cash manager; in practice, the empirical evidence does not support so extreme a position, and so some management across boundaries, be they geographic or market, seems reasonable.

Since this is an example and not a complete course on trusteeship, let us look at a typical end result rather than go through the full process of its creation.

A useful way of defining investment guidelines is by producing a grid giving proportions for investment in various areas and products; an example is shown in Table 6.1. Note that a *range* of percentages is suggested in each cell of the matrix, so that the fund manager can operate effectively; similarly, maxima are given across area by product and product by area to ensure that the overall weighting of a product or area is not excessive (or too low). These are suggested guidelines, and therefore do not add up to 100 percent.

Table 6.1   Investment grid

	Local	USA	EU	Pacific Rim	Other	Total by product
Equities	30–40%	5–15%	5–15%	0–10%	0–10%	40–70%
Govt. debt	0–10%	0–10%	0–5%	0–5%	0%	10–20%
Corp. debt	0–5%	0–10%	0%	0%	0–5%	5–15%
Property	0–5%	0%	0%	0%	0%	0–5%
Other	0–5%	0–5%	0%	0%	0%	0–10%
Total by area	45–50%	7–25%	10–15%	5–10%	5–10%	

The final area for the board to define is that of performance measures and fair associated targets. In practice, even if the first two parts of its task have been completed diligently, this aspect can be quite difficult. For example, the manager's skill in investment can only be fairly tested by comparing his or her performance with a 'naive' investment strategy based on constructing a benchmark portfolio of the same risk as that of the actual portfolio. It is then a relatively straightforward matter to create a personalised index against which investment performance can be numerically assessed. Similarly, careful policy-setting enables sensible performance measurement in other areas such as administration and cash-flow management. If they have dutifully addressed all three of these policy requirements, the trustees will have created a good framework within which to control and evaluate the performance of fund manager.

Whether it is so simple actually to *evaluate* the manager's performance, bearing in mind short- and long-term goals, is quite another matter, one which is discussed in Unit 10.

The preceding example is mostly concerned with the setting of aims and objectives and boundaries. Given the specialist nature of the subject – and the probable non-specialist skills of the board – it is reasonable that the 'expert', the fund manager, should act as designer and adviser to the board for the other points. But in the end it is the board that must consciously agree to the procedures suggested by the manager.

In particular, the remuneration structure and its linkage to performance measures needs to be very well understood by the policy-makers. Most importantly, do the performance measures align accurately with the organisation's goals? Whatever may be said, in practice, management effort will go almost exclusively towards optimising set performance measures whether or not that furthers the aims of the business. This is perfectly rational and natural behaviour for the line managers – it is the responsibility of the policy-setters to ensure that aims and measures correspond, and they should not complain about sub-optimisation if they do not.

The analogy with many other aspects of corporate risk control is, we hope, apparent and clear. The last point we should make on the subject is the reminder that the world is not static, and so neither can be the setting of risk policy. One of the significant problems seen in the business environment is that an organisation has left behind its policy guidelines. They were apposite and pertinent when they were formulated but the organisation has moved on or outgrown them. Without serious updating at best they act as a drag on the business, at worst they may put it in danger.

Before you conclude this block by looking at a real case, there is a final reading. The paper is not an easy read but it makes some interesting points, and is certainly at the cutting edge of the current management practice of risk control.

Activity 6.3 _____

Read the Steyn and Boessenkool article, '[Risk management:] Modules for standardising the process' in the Course Reader. Do not get bogged down in the detail or the mathematics; you are only trying to get a feel for what they are suggesting. It is quite a short article, but it is densely packed so it is quite likely that you will need to read it slowly and/or more than once.

In particular, think about the effort being made by the specialist treasury managers to make their esoteric information available and intelligible to the generalist policy-makers. It may not be wholly successful, but the attempt is admirable – and all too rare!

6.3   VIDEO CASE STUDY AND READING

To conclude this consideration of risk policy, you will study an example of its practical implementation in the video case study of TNT Express Worldwide, one of the world's major international courier businesses. This will be followed by a final article from the Course Reader, one which not only makes interesting points about risk management, placing it clearly in the overall context of corporate strategy, but also shows how one needs to integrate so much of finance and financial theory if one is truly to understand organisational fortune. Which, by this stage of your B821 studies, you are in a good position to do. Indeed, for some of you, better able than you perhaps realise.

Activity 6.4

Watch Video Programme 3: Packaging risk. Do please read the accompanying notes in the Audio-visual Booklet, and take a few minutes after the video to consider the points it raises. Finally, a little time spent on the 'Issues for further discussion' notes (in the Audio-visual Booklet) should provide a useful closure for this block's material.

Activity 6.5

Read the article 'Rethinking risk management', by R.M. Stultz, in the Course Reader. It ties together in an interesting way much of what you have been learning here in Block 4 with other aspects of finance from earlier in the course, for example efficient markets.

We leave you to draw your own conclusions from the article, but we would just like to make one point for you to consider while reading. In our opinion, the author could investigate more thoroughly how many of the costs involved in undertaking hedging activity are *incremental*. For example, when we discussed forex transaction risk, it became clear that the *additional* cost of booking forward compared to undertaking a spot transaction later on was negligible. If the cost of risk reduction is very small, then gaining the managerial benefits of, for example, reducing the 'noise' in performance measurement data becomes legitimate.

Lastly, far more organisations are 'closely held', using his description, than have dispersed ownership, a factor he analyses well. But much of the research data concerns large, listed companies with portfolio-minded fund managers as the typical owners. Stultz's discussion is well thought through but, in applying it, remember to think about what type of organisation you are considering.

SUMMARY

This section has returned to the concerns with which we started the block, namely the *policy* aspects of risk management. It was felt important for you to see evidence that senior managers in organisations take seriously their responsibilities in this regard, to the extent that they specifically address it in their published reports.

You also read a number of mini-case studies in the articles by Brady and Tufano; we hope these together have given you something of a feel for how these somewhat arcane techniques and products can be and are used in the real world.

The degree of detail described does vary not only with size, industry and exposure of the particular organisation but also with the opinions of the individuals concerned. Thus the levels of concern may differ between businesses, but it would still be fair to say that no responsible board – be it of directors, governors or trustees – ignores the needs of risk policy.

Moving on, we considered some generalised requirements for setting risk management policy, but since every organisation is different it was not really appropriate to give any hard and fast prescriptions. Instead, an example of pension fund trusteeship was discussed, in order to show the process of policy-setting. Of course, you should tie in the elements of this sub-section to your work on risk mapping in Unit 7 – it is an excellent information technique for aiding policy decision-making.

The Steyn and Boessenkool article was intended to show how, at the time of writing, work was being undertaken to ease the spread of understanding about treasury and risk matters beyond the confines of the finance specialism. One aspect of this is education of managers from other fields, which is an aim of B821 itself. But without a usable way of transmitting day-to-day information out of the corporate treasury *in an intelligible form,* education is unlikely to prove of much practical benefit. It is this difficult task of communicating difficult topics effectively which is being addressed by the researchers and practitioners represented by Steyn and Boessenkool.

We ended the section, the unit and the block with two activities which should exemplify the block. First, an example of overall good practice in risk management; while no one – least of all the managers themselves – would claim TNT was perfect in this regard, it certainly does represent an example which can be held up as worth emulating (with appropriate adaptation!). Then, finally, the article by Stultz which, in my opinion, serves to place risk management in its appropriate position in financial strategy, neither overly prominent nor dangerously self-effacing.

SUMMARY AND CONCLUSIONS

Block summary

Risk management is a crucial topic within business in general and finance in particular. However, it is not always the easiest of subjects with which to come to grips, whether one is talking conceptually or dealing with specific techniques. We would guess that by now this is a fact of which you are well aware! Notwithstanding this, your time studying this block should prove of considerable use over time in your career; risk is, like death, debt and taxes, always with us, so understanding and managing it must be an integral part of a Masters degree in Business Administration.

Unit 7

We started the block by discussing what was meant by risk; we all have a vernacular understanding of what it is, but it was important to clarify and be precise about what we mean by risk. For example, we noted that some forms of risk are essentially 'downside only' (e.g. health and safety, credit) but in finance we are more commonly concerned with 'symmetrical' risk, i.e. where the inherent uncertainty may lead to losses *or gains*. We also took some time to define various categories of risk.

This led us to the first important technique in the block, namely risk mapping, whereby it was intended that one derive not only measures of the separate types but also an overview of the risks impinging upon the organisation as a whole. While the mapping process is essentially one of data gathering and information extraction, which then feeds decision-making, the act of investigation itself often serves to show the need for better approaches to managing risk, as a whole and in its constituent elements. As you recall, we then left the topic of policy for the latter portion of Unit 9 – which you have very recently studied!

Having debated risk 'in the round', Unit 7 then turned to investigating interest rate risk in some depth. The first analytical method you read about was gap management, an extremely powerful technique for managing the risks created by the flows of cash through an organisation, both local and foreign.

We then moved on to discussing duration, which is a way of capturing accurately in a single measure the propensity of the value of a known stream of cash-flows to change with movements in interest rates. It gives a *weighted average maturity* for the portfolio of in- and/or out-flows; remember that the method is applicable to assets or liabilities, and, by allowing expected flows as well as certain ones, it can be extended to almost any sort of asset or liability. Durations can be used for making comparisons between, for example, assets such as fixed-rate bonds, and if you extrapolate this to an investment fund's entire portfolio, by matching the duration of the assets to that of the liabilities you can hedge away the interest rate risk. You have immunised the fund.

It was not the easiest of sections, but one way to maintain a grip on the ideas behind duration is to think of it as a further derivation of the DCF formula. In fact this is true for both the normal meaning of derivation and its strict mathematical definition. Duration is actually the first derivative of the DCF equation; doubtless you will recall that you *do not have to remember or reproduce the mathematical proof*, but it would be quite a good idea to ensure you understand the graphical explanation given in Unit 7.

Following a surfeit of theory and analysis, we then looked at some of the main products available in the financial marketplace designed to help you manage interest risk. We considered four types of product in two groups: forward rate agreements and futures, then single-currency and cross-currency swaps. The former tend to be used for dealing with particular risks in a time-frame of, roughly, 0–2 years, while swaps are typically longer-term instruments for managing the organisational debt profile. Remember also that the discussion about futures systems, e.g. the clearing house and margins, applies also to currency futures in Unit 8 and options of many sorts in Unit 9.

Unit 8

In Unit 8 we turned our attentions to two other aspects of financial risk: foreign exchange risk and trade risk. The former took up the bulk of the unit, which indicated more the technical nature of the topic rather than its being of greater importance than trade aspects. In fact it would be reasonable to say that more managers are likely to find themselves directly involved with matters of foreign exchange and credit control than with the other areas discussed in this block.

The material on foreign exchange began with an investigation of what constitutes foreign exchange risk, and three main types were identified: transaction, translation and economic exposure. The section then discussed how to measure the three forms just defined.

A crucial section followed, which looked at the mechanics of foreign exchange, describing first the size, nature and location of the foreign exchange market. Unlike, say, futures exchanges or some stock exchanges, the foreign exchange market has never (or, strictly, not for a long time) had a physical trading location; it has always been a 'virtual' market based on telephone, telex and other means of communication between the participants wherever in the city, the country or the world they happened to be.

The next section then went on to describe aspects of foreign exchange trading such as spot, cross and forward rates; the last named, it was proven, being based on interest rate differentials and not on forecasting – a key finding of the unit. The equation for relating forward margins to interest differentials was derived (the 'round the rectangle' model), and you ought to ensure that you feel comfortable about using the formula. The section concluded with a discussion of how a typical manager might need and be able to make use of the forward exchange market.

The unit continued with a look at approaches to forecasting future exchange rates, and whether or not this was a realistic proposition; if you accept that markets are even reasonably efficient, managerial effort may well be better spent analysing the impact on the organisation of various exchange rate outcomes, and what risk stance therefore to take, than in trying to outguess the market. Bearing in mind the core tenet of this block – risk management, practice and policy – the unit built on the preceding section by discussing organisational risk strategy with respect to foreign exchange risk.

This portion of Unit 8 concluded with an important section, Section 6, which looked at techniques for managing foreign exchange risk, building on the work done in the preceding part of this unit and in Unit 7.

In Section 7 we turned to discussing trade risk, including practical aspects of managing cash balances and cash flow. The material here built upon your financial analysis work in earlier parts of the course, particularly Units 2 and 3. It was not an attempt to convert all B821 students into credit analysts, so the tenor of the discussion concentrated on how generalist managers can and should involve themselves in designing and operating systems for appropriate control of cash, both when it is sitting as an account balance and when it is moving about. The section talked about, for example, simple – but crucial – rules for cash control, something which is left solely to the credit specialist at the organisation's peril.

The unit concluded with a descriptive section looking at a key tool of international business: the letter of credit. Strictly speaking, the section looked at two tools, the LC and the letter of guarantee, but the two types are close cousins and a manager is more likely to need to use the former than the latter. As with cash management, the intention is not to turn you all into documentary credit experts (there are about 150 variants of the LC alone) but to provide you with enough background and understanding so that you will know when the product is appropriate, and how to make good use of the advice of the experts!

Unit 9

Unit 9 has in structure been almost a mirror-image of Unit 7. There you began the block with a strategic level debate about what constituted risk and how to measure it, and then moved into a technical area (interest rate risk). In this unit you started with the last major technical topic of the block, options, and then concluded with a return to the subject of risk management policy.

We started Unit 9 by defining what is meant by conditional risk and financial options. Do not forget that we all use contingent claims regularly, we just call it insurance – which means very out-of-the-money put options! For example, 'putting' a burnt/flooded/subsided house on to the insurance company for the value of a new one. In Section 3 we continued the theme by introducing some of the ideas and terminology used in the options field; for example, call, put, premium, European option and American option.

The technical work really began with Section 4. This started with the very useful technique of pay-off diagrams. This is extremely powerful because the range of possible shapes needed to cover all types of basic deal is very limited, so building up the overall result of a complicated set of transactions can be achieved with little effort. Care is needed about plotting exercise prices and option premiums correctly but the resulting information is very useful.

Section 4 then continued by investigating some of the key propositions satisfied by option values; this was all leading up to Section 5, where we tackled the crucial topic of option valuation.

The main model we looked at was that invented by the two giants of option theory: the Black–Scholes model for share option valuation. We examined Robert Merton's innovation to that equation. Later in the section we investigated the adaptation of Black–Scholes designed by

Merton and also that by Garman and Kohlhagen for valuing currency options. Also a short side-step was taken to *Vital Statistics* to read about the binomial model, which is another way of considering option valuation, but one which is more difficult to implement using a spreadsheet or specialist calculator.

The section finished by asking you to read two papers – Tufano and Brady – which, between them, gave quite a range of examples of businesses using options and other derivatives.

To complete the story of the block, we returned in Section 6 to the theme of risk policy. You were introduced to this at the beginning of Unit 7 and it is appropriate that we conclude by completing the circle. You saw examples of corporate risk policy as set out in Annual Reports, and considered how, as an example, policy for a pension fund should be set by its trustees – you will study more about such matters in Unit 10. While it is almost impossible to delineate universal rules for policy-setting, you did consider some guidelines which are likely to be applicable to most if not all situations.

Finally, to put the whole block into context you studied the TNT video case and read the Stultz article. The former should have served to tie together some of the many aspects of risk management you have studied over these three units, and the latter has, we hope, placed the subject within the context of your studies of financial strategy as a whole. You should now be ready for Unit 10 to complete and provide closure to your journey through B821.

ANSWERS TO EXERCISES

Exercise 3.1 _____

(i) The option is out of the money.

Net loss = £350

(ii) The option is at the money.

Net loss = £350

(iii) The option is in the money.

Net profit = (6,500 − 6,000) − 350

= £150

Exercise 3.2 _____

See Figure A.1

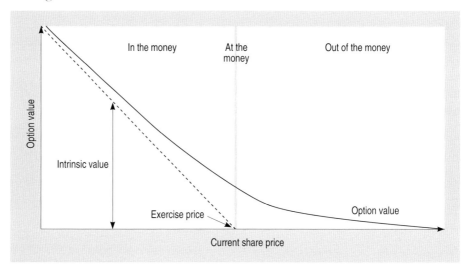

Figure A.1

Exercise 4.1 _____

| Share price at expiry date (p) | Writing 2 July 500 calls | | Buying 1 July 460 call | | Buying 1 July 540 call | | Butterfly spread |
	Gross profit (p)	Premium (p)	Gross profit (p)	Premium (p)	Gross profit (p)	Premium (p)	Net profit (p)
440	–	108	–	(73)	–	(43)	(8)
460	–	108	–	(73)	–	(43)	(8)
480	–	108	20	(73)	–	(43)	12
500	–	108	40	(73)	–	(43)	32
520	(40)	108	60	(73)	–	(43)	12
540	(80)	108	80	(73)	–	(43)	(8)
560	(120)	108	100	(73)	20	(43)	(8)

Exercise 4.2

See Figure A.2

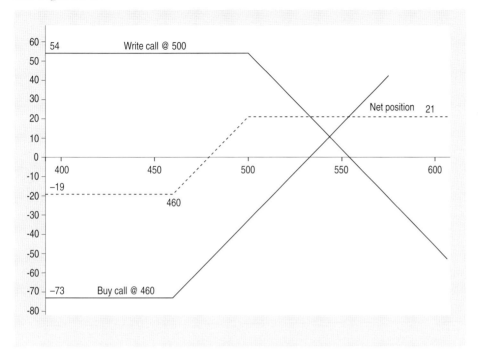

Figure A.2

Exercise 4.3

1   Nov 240 call premium at 250p is greater than share price, which contradicts Proposition 1(i).

2   The Nov 280 premium is negative, which violates Proposition 1(ii).

3   Nov 240 call premium greater than Feb 240 call premium and Feb 280 premium greater than May 280 call premium, both of which violate Proposition 2.

4   The Feb 240 call premium is lower than the Feb 260 call premium, which violates Proposition 3.

5   Two other money-making opportunities 'exist' which violate propositions which have not been given in the text:

Trade 1

Buy 1 Feb 240, 1 Feb 280 and write 2 Feb 260

Trade 2

Buy 1 May 240, 1 May 280 and write 2 May 260

Exercise 4.4

See Figure A.3

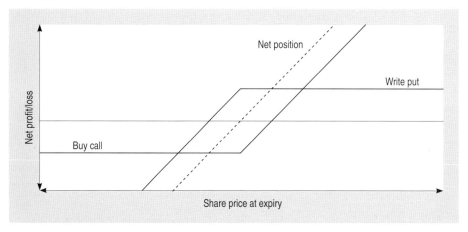

Figure A.3

While the PV(K) part of the parity equation is not immediately apparent from the pay-off diagram, the 'generic' shape is clearly the same as for holding the share, i.e. S = C – P + constant, which is just the formula rearranged.

Exercise 5.1

Using the parameter values as given, the software gives a value for the call option of 26.20p (the percentage figure is the same as S = 100). Note that this is only a little higher than the intrinsic value of 25p; an option that is so far in the money has little downside protection. S can fall all the way to 75 before the safety net kicks in.

Using the option valuation software, look at the difference of estimating the price of the call using 60 day maturity (26.2437p) and 58 day maturity (26.2006p).

Exercise 5.2

With exercise price = 1.7000, t = 2.25/12 = 0.1875 (67.5 days), and other parameters as before, the put option value is 3.27 cents. This compares with 3.35 in Table 5.1; in fact using a volatility figure of 10.27% (10.40 for the Merton model) would match the market result.

Exercise 6.1

It is probably due to the different importance of foreign business as a proportion of total revenues. Boots is dominated by its UK business, naturally denominated in sterling. In the note quoted it states that 'modest sales and purchases are made in a range of currencies'; the company probably regards the cost of instigating a system for forward hedging as not justified by the small scale of the amounts at risk.

Blue Circle, in contrast, has substantial businesses overseas, and thus regards the risk of forex fluctuations as sufficiently high as to justify a hedging process.

APPENDIX PROOFS OF PROPOSITIONS CONCERNING OPTION VALUATION

This Appendix refers to the propositions concerning option valuation as discussed in Section 4.2.

Proposition 1

The premium of a call option is:

(i)   less than or equal to the current price of the underlying security;

(ii) greater than or equal to the difference between the price of the underlying security and the exercise price;

(iii) non-negative.

Or in mathematical terms:

$$S \geqslant C \geqslant \max(0, S - K)$$

where $\max(0, S - K)$ denotes the maximum of 0 and $(S - K)$; and S = current share price; C = call premium; K = exercise price.

Proof

(i) We first prove that the call price is less than or equal to the current share price. We do this by assuming the opposite, i.e. $C > S$, and show that this leads to an arbitrage opportunity.

Combination: Buy a share and write a call on it; according to our assumption this yields a positive amount.

Subsequently:

(a) Before the expiry date: if the call is exercised against you, you get the exercise price and deliver the share so that you get a positive amount of $(C + K - S)$. This must be positive as $C > S$.

(b) Expiry date and after: if the call expires unexercised you are left with the share, which cannot have a negative price.

You thus end up with a non-negative amount (increased possibly by any dividends paid). Hence the assumption $C > S$ leads to an arbitrage opportunity and, since we reject the feasibility of such opportunities, the opposite must actually be true, i.e. $S \geqslant C$.

(ii) Again, assume that the opposite of what needs to be proved is true, i.e. $(S - K) > C$.

Combination: Buy the call, exercise it and sell the stock: the net amount received is $S - K - C$, which on our assumption is positive. There is no further step, as the position is liquidated.

Hence the assumption leads to an arbitrage opportunity, and the opposite must be true or $C \geqslant S - K$.

Strictly speaking this proof is only correct for an American option, as it requires immediate exercise of the option, but an equivalent proof – though more complicated and involving the short sale of the share and investing the proceeds – can be made for the European type.

Proposition 2

For the same exercise price and share, the price of a call option increases as the time to expiry increases,.

Proof

Again assume the opposite, for example that the Jul 500 call is priced below the Apr 500 call.

Combination: Buy a Jul 500 call and write a Apr 500 call, giving you a positive amount now.

Subsequently:

(i) Up to Apr expiry: if the Apr 500 is exercised against you, exercise the Jul 500 and you are no worse off (you obtain the share by paying 500p and pass it on at 500p). Alternatively, the Apr option lapses.

(ii) After Apr expiry, you are left with the Jul option, which cannot have a negative price.

You thus end in either case with a non-negative amount. Hence the assumption holds for an arbitrage opportunity, which completes the proof. Again, the simple form of the proof is really only true for an American option, but an equivalent proof can be produced for a European option.

Proposition 3

For the same expiry date, the prices of call options decrease as their exercise prices increase.

Proof

Again assume the opposite, for example that the Jul 500 has a higher price than the Jul 460.

Combination: Buy a Jul 460 call and write a Jul 500 call, which gives you a positive amount now.

Subsequently:

(i) At or before Jul expiry: if the 500 call is exercised against you, exercise your own call, so that you end up with 500 – 460 = 40p a share. Otherwise the 500 call lapses.

(ii) At Jul expiry, Jul 500 not exercised against you: you are left with the Jul 460 call, which cannot have a negative price. Thus an arbitrage opportunity has been created, which completes the proof.

Proposition 4

If there is no ex-dividend date until after the time to expiry, American call options should not be exercised until expiry, and the value of an American call option is the same as that of an equivalent European call option.

Proof

This is very straightforward. If there are no cash flows during the option's life to which you become entitled by actual share ownership, then there can be no advantage to early exercise as it would destroy the benefit of downside protection given by the option without offering any countervailing gain. Thus there is no value to the early exercise characteristic of an American option, and its value is the same as for a European contract with the same exercise terms.

Proposition 5

For European options without dividends, the value of a put option is equal to the value of an otherwise identical call option minus the current share price plus the present value of the exercise price for the put (or the call), i.e:

$$P = C - S + PV(K)$$

So, once the value of a call option or a put option is known, the value of the other (provided it has the same exercise price and time to expiry) can be found from Proposition 5.

The proof of this proposition follows directly from the fact that the two portfolios of (i) the share and the put, and (ii) the call and the present value of the exercise price have exactly the same pay-off at the expiry date – hence the two portfolios must have the same price now. The following table brings this out, where S = the current price of the share; S_1 = the price of the share at expiry; K = the exercise price; and PV(K) = the present value of the exercise price at expiry.

A worked example of this proof is given in *Vital Statistics*, Section 5.7.3.

Table A1   Pay-off at expiry

	If $S_1 > K$	If $S_1 < K$
Portfolio A		
Own share	S_1	S_1
Own put	0	$K - S_1$
Total	S_1	**K**
Portfolio B		
Own call	$S_1 - K$	0
Invest PV(K)	K	K
Total	S_1	**K**

Thus, the value of a put option can be determined from the value of a call option *plus* the present value of the exercise price *minus* the share price.

REFERENCES

Aczel, M. (1987) 'Updating option valuation systems', *Euromoney*, November.

Cox, J., Ross, S. and Rubinstein, M. (1979) 'Option pricing, a simplified approach', *Journal of Financial Economics*, September, pp. 229–63.

Garman, M. and Kohlhagen, S. (1983) 'Foreign currency option values', *Journal of International Money and Finance*, 2, pp. 231–7.

Hull, J. (1995) *Introduction to Futures and Options Markets*, 2nd ed, Prentice Hall International.

Merton, R. C. (1973) On the theory of rational option pricing, *Bell Journal of Economics and Management Science*, vol. 4 (Spring), pp. 141–183.

Ross, D., Clark, I. and Taiyeb, S. (1987) *International Treasury Management*, Woodhead-Faulkner.

Ross, S. A., Westerfield, R. W. and Jaffe, J. (1996) *Corporate Finance*, 4th ed, Irwin McGraw Hill.

Taylor, F. (1996) *Mastering Derivatives Markets*, Pitman.

ACKNOWLEDGEMENTS

Grateful acknowledgement is made to the following sources for permission to reproduce material in this unit:

Text

Pp. 39–41: Annual Report and Accounts 1997, Boots Company PLC; pp. 42–44: Blue Circle Annual Report, Blue Circle Industries PLC; pp. 44–45: Annual Report and Accounts 1997, Carlton Communications.

Cartoons/Photographs

P. 8: © Tony Stone Images; p. 9: © PowerStock/Zefa; pp. 24 and 48: © 1998 by Sidney Harris; p. 30: © Associated Press; pp. 36 and 53: Roger Beale, from the *Financial Times*; p. 30: © 1990 by Sidney Harris – *Harvard Business Review*.

B821 FINANCIAL STRATEGY